YOU CAN'T MAKE THIS UP ...

LIFE of the Cussing Pastor's Daughter

DOMONIQUE MATTHEWS

Worldwide Kingdom Publishing
P.O. Box 2722
Southfield, Michigan 48034
313-544-8010

Website: www.worldwidekp.net

ISBN: 978-1-934905-91-3

Printed in the United States of America

Domonique Matthews & Thaddeus Matthews

<u>DEDICATION</u>

To every woman who grew up without her father — this book is for you.

To the women whose relationships with their fathers have been strained or toxic — I pray that within these pages, you find healing, peace, and restoration.

To the Daddy's girls, may you always cherish and protect the rare and beautiful bond you share.

Finally, to my father, the late great Pastor Thaddeus Matthews — this is for you. I will continue to carry your legacy through me. I miss you deeply, always.

SPECIAL THANKS

To my sons, Kion and Jaxson — you are my strength, my motivation, my everything. You are always at the center of my thoughts, guiding every decision I make. I pray I make you proud to call me your mother. I love you both, deeply and endlessly.

To my praying mother, I see you. I am you and I love you more than words can say.

To my Golden Girls — my big sister Katrina, my best cousin Shanika, and my best friend Mauri — thank you. Thank you for letting me be fully and unapologetically me. Thank you for listening to me cry, letting me vent about the same things on repeat, and lovingly keeping me in check. Your love and support mean more than you'll ever know.

INTRODUCTION

Do you love your father? Are you a Daddy's girl? Is your father your hero? This book tells a different kind of story — the journey of a woman who didn't meet her father until later in life. Through these pages, Domonique Matthews opens her heart to share her trials, tribulations, and ultimate triumphs. She speaks candidly about the pain of absence, the weight of unanswered questions, and the power of forgiveness that led to healing. Even in moments of deep adversity and public humiliation, she held on to hope — hope that God would one day restore what was broken, and He did. You will laugh. You will cry, and more than anything, you will be reminded of the strength that comes from faith, love, and reconciliation.

This is more than just a story, it's a testimony of a daughter's journey back to her father. A woman's journey back to herself. May you be inspired, uplifted, and healed as you walk through these pages with the daughter of the late Pastor Thaddeus Matthews — Domonique Matthews.

TABLE OF CONTENTS

Dedication
Special Thanks
Introduction

Thaddeus Matthews & Domonique Matthews

Chapter One
WHO'S YO DADDY?

Growing up, our house was always full. It was full of voices, footsteps, and names that didn't quite match. There was me, my mom, my older sister, two step-sisters, a brother, and the man I called, "Dad". At the time, I didn't question why we all had different last names. I saw it, but it didn't seem strange. My world was shaped by the people around me, not the names they carried. My sister, nine years older, was my closest companion in the house, and my stepdad; although I didn't know he was a stepdad then, was simply "Dad" to me. I remember TeTe, my biological father's adopted mother. She passed away when I was still young, but her funeral left a lasting impression on me. I didn't know most of the people there, but I remember walking down the front row, hugging everyone like I had known them all my life. It felt like the right thing to do, even if I didn't understand who they were.

After the service, something happened that I'll never forget. In the parking lot of the church, a man dressed in all white approached me. He smiled, reached into his pocket, and handed me a crisp twenty-dollar bill. I didn't know who he was, but at that moment, he was the kindest man I had ever met. I was thrilled, because twenty dollars felt like a fortune. For days afterward, I couldn't stop talking about him. "The man who gave me the twenty dollars?" I'd say over and over. I wanted to see him again; because really, I wanted another $20. At that age, twenty dollars felt like magic. But I didn't question who he was or why he gave it to me. Just like I never questioned who the man was in our house. To me, my stepdad was my "Dad." That was the truth I lived in, and I didn't need anything more.

My mama was a beautiful woman. She had long, flowing black hair, always wore her makeup just right, and never let her nails go undone. To me, she was the definition of elegance. As a little girl, I wanted nothing more than to be just like her—graceful, confident, and pretty.

One day, I was playing in her makeup while she had emptied her purse onto the bed. Lipsticks, receipts, keys, and other little treasures were scattered across the covers. That's when I saw it, a folded piece of paper that looked important. I picked it up, curious, and unfolded it. It was my birth certificate. I didn't know why, but I felt drawn to read it. To my surprise here it was: **Mother – Gina Matthews. Father – Thaddeus Matthews.** My name— **Domonique Matthews**—was right there, too. For the first time, I realized my mother and I shared the same last name. However, the name that stood out the most was one I didn't recognize: **Thaddeus Matthews.** I asked, "Who is Thaddeus Matthews?" It wasn't the first time I had questions. I had already been asking about the man in white who gave me twenty dollars at TeTe's funeral. Now, with this new name in front of me, my questions could not be ignored. My mama looked at me, and I could tell something shifted in her eyes. That was the moment she decided it was time to talk. One day, while riding in the car with my mom, she told me something that would change the way I saw my world. "You're going to meet a man today," she said, "He is your biological father; but he is not your father." Her words were careful, almost rehearsed, as if she wanted to make sure I understood that the man I called "Dad" at home was still the one who mattered the most.

We pulled into the parking lot of CK's Coffee Shop on Highland Street. That's where we were meeting him for breakfast. I didn't know what to expect, but I remember feeling uneasy. When we walked in, I saw him right away. He was a heavyset man dressed in all black, wearing combat boots like he was some kind of security guard or police officer. Big rings covered his fingers, and when he spoke, his voice was loud and commanding. He didn't sound like a stranger trying to connect; he sounded like someone who was use to being in control. My mom was visibly irritated. I could feel the tension between them before they even said a word. I sat quietly, watching them talk, not saying much myself. I had already made up my mind. The way my mom had framed it, this man might be my biological father, but he was not my *dad;* and sitting there in that booth, I felt it in my gut: *He is not fit to replace the dad I have at home.*

That breakfast at CK's was the first and last time I saw him for years. Whatever connection might have been possible did not take root that day. I left with more questions then answers, but also with a stronger sense of who I considered family.

Years passed before I saw him again. Then one day, while I was at the Mall of Memphis with my older sister who at that time, had to take me everywhere she went; we ran into him, my biological father. He greeted me with a big hug, like he was genuinely excited to see me. It caught me off guard. We made small talk, the kind you have when you're trying to bridge years of silence. Then he asked, "Is there anything in this mall that you want?" Coming from a home where money was tight, I never expected a question like that from him. I had never owned a pair of Jordans before, but I told him there were some shoes I wanted! What I didn't say was that they were a $200 pair of Jordans. Still, we walked together to Foot Locker, and to my surprise, he bought them for me. They were white and black with a little gold, I think they were Jordan Fours. I remember holding the box like it was treasure. He gave me another big hug before we parted ways, and just like that, he was gone again. I wouldn't see him for years after that. But I never forgot that moment. Not just because of the shoes, but because it was one of the few times he showed up and it really mattered.

Growing up in Orange Mound, everybody had that one auntie, whose house was the weekend spot for all the kids. For me, that was my Auntie's house. It was where we laughed, played, and stayed up too late. It was also where I started to learn more about the parts of my life that had been kept from me. I found out that I was being protected from seeing my father. My auntie did not like that at all. She believed I had a right to know him, even if he wasn't perfect. So on weekends when I stayed at her house, she started calling him. "Come by and see your daughter," she would say and sometimes, he did. He never took me anywhere. He would just stop by, sit for a bit, and catch up. He would hand me a few dollars, just enough for the candy lady and then he was gone. It wasn't much. It wasn't what I needed. But it was something.

By then, I gradually understood: this man was my biological father. Not because anyone sat me down and explained it again, but because the pieces were starting to fit together. The man from CK's. The man from the mall. The man who stopped by Auntie's house with candy money. They were all the same person, and still, somehow, he felt like a stranger.

In Orange Mound, weekends at my auntie's house were legendary. Her home was the place where kids gathered, music played loud, and the smell of fried food drifted from the kitchen like a warm invitation. It was a place of joy, laughter, and freedom. That's where the cousin started showing up. He wasn't a close family member, just a distant cousin who suddenly became a regular. He was in his twenties, older than the rest of us, but he fit right in. He had a bright yellow Ford Explorer that looked like it came straight out of a music video. He was funny, charismatic, and always had a story to tell. The kind of cousin everyone wanted to be around. He brought energy with him. He was big, bold, and magnetic. The younger kids looked up to him. The older ones laughed at his jokes. The adults didn't seem to mind him hanging around. He was the "cool cousin," the one who made everything feel a little more exciting when he walked through the door. At first, I was just happy to be included, to be noticed. I was happy to be around someone who made the room light up. Unfortunately, sometimes the brightest lights cast the darkest shadows. I was in the seventh grade just a girl, really; but my body told a different story. I had curves that made people look twice, and a maturity that made them assumed I understood things, but I didn't. My sister and I were nine years apart, and I always wanted to be like her. I wore her clothes not to be grown, but because I could. That day, I didn't think twice when he asked me to ride with him to drop someone off. I didn't feel unsafe. I didn't feel unsure. Not yet. But then, in the car, he turned to me and said, "You know we ain't real cousins, right?" I laughed, confused. "What do you mean?" He brushed it off with a grin, like it was a joke. But something about the way he said it made my stomach twist. He explained that my uncle had never married his mom, that they'd just been together for years. Technically, we were not family. It was the first time I felt a shift, like the ground beneath me had moved just slightly, but enough to make me feel unsteady. I didn't have the words for it then, but I felt it. A warning! A whisper in my gut that something was not right. He said he needed to stop by his house. I didn't question it. I was young. I was trusting. I was still seeing him through the lens of who I thought he was. I remembered he needed to go by his house for a quick stop, a house I had never been to. I remember driving in Orange Mound going through a tunnel on to Southern

Street. He went to his house and told me I could come in. Now, I was very naive and young, because I was comfortable and cool with this cousin. I did not realize at the time, he was grooming me. He took me to his house and told me to get comfortable. Then he started to show me around his house. He showed me high tech equipment and a big screen tv and we landed in his bedroom. Then I grab the remote and started going through channels. I remember laying across his bed just waiting for him to finish, whatever he needed to stop by there for. Whatever I was watching had my attention, and he came and joined in on his bed. Somehow it seemed we both were laying very comfortably in his bed when the touching started. It started slowly just caressing, then hands going lower. I remember it feeling weird and me feeling frozen. He slid his hands down into my pants and began putting his fingers inside me. I remember it being painful, and something in me died. I felt disgusted, embarrassed, ashamed, uncomfortable. Remember feeling like I would get in trouble, no one could ever know. Did I bring this on myself? Was every whisper I had heard about myself true? I got the courage to say "STOP" and maybe it was the tone. He did not force anything. I think he knew he had crossed the line. A line that I could never go back too. My innocence was taken. He took me back to my auntie's house. Apparently, we had been gone too long, or maybe it was the shame written on my face that I was trying to hide, when someone told me to get my "Fast Ass" in the house. Now that I think of it, something must had been giving everyone a vibe, because he always wanted me to ride with him, and usually I would tell my cousins. Hey y'all come on let's ride. Unfortunately, this day it was just me. I remember getting back and my cousins started teasing me, singing I was his girlfriend and that I liked him. I was constantly screaming, getting mad as hell, saying "No he's not!" I remember feeling like I just wanted my momma, my safe place. Because my sister and I were nine years apart, and my step sisters and step brother were only over every now and then, and holidays. Often, I would spend a lot of time by myself in my room, and I used to write in my diary. I would write what I did in my entire day in my diary. Needless to say, I wrote about that day in my diary. Suddenly, at a friend's sleepover my mother had abruptly called my friend's mother, and said, "Domonique has to come home and she has to come home now!" I used to hide the diary in my top panty drawer, and for some reason I never actually knew, my mom found my diary and read everything. Through reading, my mother learned of that day. I was confronted about it, but I don't remember much being done about it. I heard whispers that my Mom confronted him about it, but really nothing. I erased that day, and those feelings, so far away that I completely had forgotten about it. He disappeared and I wouldn't see him again until I was a grown woman. It didn't hit me until I was a 35 years old woman, sitting on a therapist's couch when she asked "When was the first time you ever felt unprotected?"

Dear Younger Me,

I'm so sorry. I'm sorry you had to carry so much on your little shoulders. I'm sorry that the people who were supposed to protect you didn't. You deserved to feel safe. You deserved to be held, to be heard, and to be loved without conditions.

I know you were scared. I know you felt alone. I know you wondered if it was your fault, but it wasn't. None of it was. You were just a child, trying to survive in a world that didn't always feel kind.
But I want you to know something now:
You are not broken.
You are not invisible.
You are not what happened to you.
You are strong. You are worthy. You are still here and that means something. That means you've already survived so much, and you are still becoming someone powerful, someone beautiful, someone whole.

I see you now. I love you now and I promise to keep protecting you, even if no one else does.
You didn't deserve the pain, but you do deserve the healing and I'm walking with you every step of the way.

With all the love,
You should've had back then,
Me!

Chapter Two

TRAPPED

Moving from Orange Mound to East Memphis felt like stepping into a whole new world. The streets were quieter, the houses a little bigger, and the air just felt... different. I wasn't sure how I would fit in, but life has a funny way of surprising you. My next-door neighbor was the first person I really connected with. He was a boy, but our bond was more like siblings than anything else. We hung out on the porch, talk about school, music, and life. One day, he leaned over and said, "You know that boy who's always riding his bike around with the basketball? He's got a crush on you." I laughed it off at first until I saw him. He was tall, like 5'10', which was a lot for me. His skin was this smooth, pretty brown, and his smile was bright white and impossible to ignore. He always had that backpack slung over one shoulder, and I later found out it only had two things in it: a jar of Vaseline and a basketball. He kept his arms shiny like he was always ready for a photo shoot. Said it made his "muscles" pop. I thought it was hilarious and kind of cute. I started going to the local gym with my girlfriends, pretending we were just there to watch the games. But really, I was only watching him. The way he moved on the court, the way he laughed with his friends, it all had me hooked.

One day, after a game, we were hanging out near the bleachers. He looked at me, grinned, and said, "You're gonna have my baby one day." He was joking at least I thought he was, but my heart skipped a beat anyways. I didn't know what the future held, but in that moment, I knew one thing for sure: this boy with the shiny arms and the basketball had just made my world a whole lot more interesting. At sixteen, I thought I knew what love was supposed to feel like. Butterflies in your stomach, long walks home, someone who made you feel seen. Maybe if my father had been there, maybe I would not have fallen for the first boy that showed me attention. But hey! For a while, that is what it felt like with him. Every morning, I would stop by the candy lady's house, his house and he'd be waiting, ready to walk me to school. After school, he would be right there again, like clockwork. It became our thing. Our routine. Then the words started coming more often. "You're gonna have my baby." At first, I laughed it off. "I mean, who says that?" But he kept saying it and then it wasn't just jokes anymore. It was pressure. "If you love me, you'll do it. You don't want to lose me, do you?" I was being pressured to have sex or lose him. I was still a virgin. I had never even had a real conversation about sex with my parents. I didn't know what I was doing, and honestly, I didn't feel ready. But I was scared—scared of losing him, scared of being alone, scared of disappointing someone I thought I cared about. So I gave in and when it happened, it wasn't like the movies. There were no fireworks, no magic. Just confusion. I didn't feel special. I didn't feel closer to him. I just felt...different. Like something had shifted inside me, and I wasn't sure how to name it. This boy and I were *everything* to each other. We were always together laughing, walking, and talking about life like we had it all figured out. However, deep down, we both knew things were about to change. He was leaving for college in Denver, Colorado. I was getting ready for my senior year, still holding tight to my dream of going to TSU—Tennessee State University. I wanted to be a Tigerette so bad. I could already picture myself dancing on the field at the Southern Heritage Classic, the crowd cheering, and the band playing. That was my dream, and I was chasing it with everything I had within me. Even with all that excitement, my heart felt heavy. His mom was planning a surprise going-away party, and I was helping like everything was normal, but it wasn't. We were about to be in two different places, living two different lives and even though we said we'd make it work, I couldn't help but wonder if our love was strong enough to stretch across all those miles. He used to say, "You're gonna have my baby," like it was a promise. Like no matter where life took us, we'd always find our way back to each other. I didn't know how to respond to that. I was still figuring out who I was, still scared to talk to my mama about anything close to sex. Not because she wouldn't listen, I knew she always made space for me; but, because I didn't know how to say the words out loud. I didn't know how to explain the feelings I didn't fully understand.

I remember vividly while his mom was getting everything ready for his surprise going away party, she told me my job was to keep him out of the house and keep him busy. After we spent so long of time, walking around the neighborhood, visiting friends; we ended up at my house, where no one was home and we ended up having sex. We were so young and dumb that we were having unprotected sex and playing what they called "The Pullout Game!" In the midst of having sex, he said, "You're going to have my baby! I told him, "Do not cum inside me!" As I grew nervous, it was getting good to him, and he pinned my arms back really strong where I couldn't push him off me. My body began to resist him, and I continued to repeat, "Don't cum in me," nervously. He used his body being on top of me to hold me down while he penetrated all inside me.

After he was finished, I just laid there and tears began to fall rolling from my eyes to my ears. As I laid there only looking up at the ceiling, not being able to look him in his face, I was in total disbelief. Knowing that it was now a huge chance that I was pregnant and it was no turning back. He began to constantly kiss me on my cheeks and on my forehead saying, "I am going to take care of you!" More like in a panic, and that he knew he had messed up, as well. I remember feeling so violated and so pissed off by his actions. Filled with so much regret, and feeling so stupid. This was a familiar place for me just like my past experience I was embarrassed, and I felt ashamed. Placing the blame only on myself and resulting to my coping methods, like anything else: I acted like nothing had happened.

We went on to his surprise "Going Away Party" and we had just finished playing games and laughing with his cousins and aunties, and I was feeling kinda ok, like maybe I could forget for a second feeling, "violated." Then they told him to give a speech. I thought he was just gonna say thank you and maybe crack a joke or two. But no! He stood up, all confident, and started thanking everybody for coming. I was smiling, thinking, "Aww, look at him being all grown." Then out of nowhere, he said, "I'm gonna be at school doing my work, getting my education, and on the phone with my girlfriend and when I come back, I hope my girlfriend is pregnant!" Then he ran out the room. Y'all, my jaw dropped! This muthafucka! My eyes got big as quarters. I was frozen. His mama, his grandma, his aunties, *everybody* turned and looked straight at me like I had just grown a baby bump right there in the living room. They started asking, "Are you pregnant? Are you pregnant?" I couldn't even speak. I just stood there like a deer in headlights. I wanted the floor to open up and swallow me whole. At that moment, I realized he wasn't just playing. He was serious. He had been saying it for months, but now he said it out loud, in front of his whole family. Because of what had happened earlier that day, I knew deep down, he might have gotten exactly what he wanted. I felt embarrassed. Like *so* embarrassed. But I also felt trapped. Like I didn't even have control over my own story anymore and I didn't know how to tell anyone what I was really feeling.

When he left for school, it felt like the end of the world. We were crying on the phone, texting non-stop, acting like we were never gonna survive being apart. I couldn't sleep. I couldn't eat. I missed him so bad it hurt. It was puppy love. But, when he came home for break, something was different. Everything he did, started to get on my nerves. The way he talked, the way he joked, even the way he looked at me. I didn't know what was wrong with me. I thought maybe I was just being moody, but deep down, I knew I was changing. I was growing. For the first time, I didn't like how he made me feel. He kept saying, "You're gonna have my baby. I know you're pregnant. I just know it's a girl." I was like, "*Boy, what?*" I started standing up for myself more. I told him I didn't want a baby. I told him I had dreams. I wanted to leave Memphis, go to college, dance at TSU, live my life. I was finally starting to say it out loud. But then... weird stuff started happening. I couldn't stand the smell of my own bathroom. Every time I brushed my teeth, I'd gag like crazy. I thought something was wrong with the pipes or maybe there was mold or something. I even knocked on my mama's door like, "Can I use your bathroom? Mine smells weird." She looked at me like I was crazy. Then came the cramps. Outta nowhere. Sharp, random, and strong enough to bring me to my knees. I didn't know what was going on. I was so young, I didn't even know my own body. My mama thought maybe it was a bladder infection. But deep down... I was starting to wonder. By the time I was getting sick every day in third period, I knew something wasn't right. My teacher even started bringing me crackers, like I was some little old lady with morning sickness. I didn't even put two and two together. I just thought maybe I was stressed or had a weak stomach or something. Then came that Sunday, me and my sister went to church, and afterward we hit up Rafferty's. I ordered salmon, which I *never* do, and the second I ate it, I had to run to the bathroom. I came back to the table pale and shaky, and my sister just looked at me like *"Girl..."* Then she hit me with it: **"Do you think you might be pregnant?"** I frozed. I said, "I don't know." But honestly, I hadn't even thought about it. I was too young to know what my body was trying to tell me.

The next school day, Tuesday, I got sick again in the third period. That was it! I texted my sister: **"I think we need to check and see if I'm pregnant."** She texted back, **"Meet you at mom's house."** She beat me there. That's how nervous she was. I changed into this pink velour jogging suit with a white crop top, still had the perfect stomach, no bump, no signs. I didn't look pregnant. I didn't *feel* pregnant. I just felt... scared! When I walked in, my mama was vacuuming, and out of nowhere she said, **"You know you can go to Planned Parenthood to get birth control pills."** I swear I almost passed out. I was like, *"Oh my God, she knows!"* I still don't know how or why she said that, but it felt like she could see right through me. Well, we went to Planned Parenthood. My sister paid for everything. I took the urine test and sat in the waiting room. My heart was pounding, hands sweating, and I was trying not to cry. I kept thinking, *"What if I am? What if I'm not? What happens next?"* I could see the lady walking over to the counter, dropping the little stick into the cup like it was just another Tuesday. Then she said, "Whoo!" Like she was talking to herself, but I heard it loud and clear. My heart dropped. I looked at her with these big, sad puppy eyes and asked, barely above a whisper, "Am I pregnant?" She didn't even hesitate, **"14 weeks."** That was it. No soft voice. No warning. Just *14 weeks*. I dropped my head. I couldn't even cry. I was too scared.

My whole body felt numb, like I wasn't even in the room anymore. A thousand thoughts started racing through my mind all at once. *How? When? What am I gonna do? What is Mama gonna say?* I couldn't believe this was actually happening to me. I thought about my mama, how she had my sister at 16. I thought about my sister, pregnant at 16, too. Now me, 16 and pregnant. I felt like I had just fallen into some kind of cycle, I swore I was gonna break. I had dreams. I had plans. I was supposed to be a Tigerette at TSU, dancing in the Southern Heritage Classic, not sitting in a clinic hearing I was 14 weeks pregnant.

I now found myself trying to make a decision on whether to keep my baby or have an abortion. My sister was ride or die as usual, "You know I got you, if you want to keep the baby or if you choose to have an abortion. I will take care of it." My brain was feeling like an empty room. I decided to call him, and tell him, "I am pregnant." He was so excited! Like I felt like he started running through his house. I told him that I was going to have an abortion, because I was not ready to have a kid. You could hear his excitement come all the way down. Having a child right now was not in my plans. I was still a kid myself. This was not what I wanted and I told him that. In sure panic, he called his mother to give her the news, that I was indeed pregnant, but I wasn't keeping it. Begging her to talk me out of it and she did just that, but she also comfort a little scared girl, who entire life was about to change. She encourage me that I wasn't alone in this, and that the sin was in the sex, but my baby was a blessing from God. She was right! I look at my sister, who understood the assignment, "How am I going to tell Momma?" With complete fear all over my face, I knew I couldn't do this alone, I needed backup. I called in the troops: my sister, my step-sister, and a whole lot of courage I didn't even know I had. Mama had no idea why the house was suddenly full of people. She was just doing her usual, walking around, cleaning, talking like everything was normal. Then my sister blurted out, "Mama, you're going be a grandma again!" Mama froze. She looked at Trina and said, "Trina, are you pregnant again?" Trina laughed and said, "Nawh, not me!" Then Mama turned to Cordia, my step-sister. "Cordia, are you pregnant?" Cordia was cracking up, "No ma'am, not me!" Mama looked around, confused. "Well who is it then? I *know* Domonique not pregnant!" Trina, trying to lighten the mood but still serious, said, "Well mama, who's left?" That's when Mama turned and looked at me. Her face changed. She had this soft, sad look in her eye like she was hoping with everything within her that the answer was, no! Like she already knew, but didn't want it to be true. Then she asked, real calm, "Domonique... are you pregnant?" I couldn't even look her in the eyes. I just whispered, "Fourteen weeks." And y'all... she *fell out* screaming like the actress, Jada Pinkett Smith in the movie Kingdom Come, "Lord, Take Me Now!" Like literally, my strong, no-nonsense mama just dropped to the floor. I had never seen her like that before. My heart was pounding so hard I thought it was gonna break through my chest. I felt like I had disappointed her, like I had broken something we couldn't fix.

When my stepdad came in and Mama told him I was pregnant, he didn't say a word, he just punched the wall. *Boom.* I jumped. My heart dropped. I felt like I had ruined everything. Like I had let everybody down. I remember thinking, *"Dang... I done pissed the whole family off."* My real dad was nowhere to be found. Like always.

Now that the secret was out, it was like everything changed. Mama stopped talking to me as much. She wasn't mean, just very distant. She was quiet and I could feel the disappointment in the air, even when nobody said anything. I knew she was probably embarrassed. We were already struggling, and now I had added another mouth to feed. My stepdad never had a steady job, one minute he was washing cars at the lot, the next he was laid off again. We moved so much, I was in a different school every year. I was used to instability, but this situation was a whole new level.

We made the decision to keep the baby. I thought maybe —*just maybe*—that would motivate him, to step up, stay in school, and do better. But nope. Two days after we said we were keeping the baby, he was on a Greyhound bus back to Memphis. Dropped out of college just like that.

When he got off that bus, I barely recognized him. He wasn't the clean-cut boy with the shiny muscles anymore. He looked like a whole different person. Hair grown out, pants sagging, smelling like weed. I just stared at him like, *"What happened to you?"* He had gone to Denver and got caught up. They had just legalized weed out there, and instead of focusing on school, he was partying, smoking, doing whatever. Now he was back. No degree. No plan. Just back and I was standing there, 16 years old, pregnant, and realizing that I was about to do this *mostly* on my own. We were broken up by then, he cheated on me, just like that. I started my senior year in high school *pregnant*, and he was out here wildin'out. He wasn't the same person anymore. He was dating all these girls, and the worst part: he would tell every single one of them that he had a pregnant girlfriend; like it was some kind of badge of honor. So of course, I had girls calling my phone, playing on it, texting me with nonsense. I was already stressed, already tired, and now I had to deal with *that* too. My dad, we weren't even talking. The last memory I had of him was him buying me a Cricket phone, then yelling at me when I told him the bill needed to be paid. Like, *sir, you gave me the phone!* It had been years since I had seen or talked to him. I didn't even know if he knew I was pregnant. But something in me still wanted him to be there. I wanted him to care. So I called him. We made small talk at first. "How are you doing? How have you been?" Then I said, "I'm pregnant… and I'm about to have my baby shower. I wanted to know if you would like to come?" There was this long silence. I could feel the disappointment through the phone. Then he finally said, **"I don't celebrate kids out of wedlock."** That was it and that is all he had to say. I was so stunned. I said, "That's it? Is that all you have to say to me?" He said nothing else. Just silence. I remember holding the phone, my hands shaking, my heart hurting. I felt so stupid for even calling. He hadn't checked on me in *years*, and the one time I reached out, hoping for something—*anything*—he shut me down. Then I remembered the last time I saw him. It was at this local car lot where all the old heads used to hang out, playing checkers and talking trash. My stepdad used to wash cars there. I walked into the lobby, and one of the men said, **"Thaddeus, there goes your daughter."** Without even blinking, he said, "That's not my daughter. That's Danny Bell's daughter." I didn't say a word. I just stood there. My heart sank. I never forgot that moment. Even now, if I close my eyes, I can still feel that rejection. Like a bruise that never fully healed.

So we went on to have the baby shower and let me tell you, it was awkward. Like, *really* awkward. Two people who couldn't stand each other, standing in the same room, pretending to celebrate a baby we made together. Everybody knew we weren't on good terms. It was so obvious that his own brother got up and sang **"We Can't Be Friends"** by Deborah Cox. I wanted to disappear into the floor.

Hey love,

I know it hurts. This kind of emptiness that comes from someone who should be there but isn't—it's hard to explain to anyone who hasn't felt it. You might wonder if something's wrong with you, or if you did something to deserve the silence. But let me tell you this loud and clear: it's not your fault. It was never your fault.

A father's absence says more about him than it ever will about you. You are not less worthy of love, attention, or protection just because, he didn't show up the way he should have. But here's the beautiful part:

You still get to write your story.

You still get to define your worth.

You still get to build a life full of love, even if it didn't start that way. Surround yourself with people who do show up for you—your mom, your siblings, your friends, your teachers, your mentors, or even your future self. Let their love remind you that you are not alone.

When the pain creeps in and it will sometimes, don't be afraid to feel it. But don't let it define you. Let it fuel you. Let it push you to become the kind of person who breaks cycles, who loves deeply, and who never lets anyone feel the way you did.

You are strong. You are valuable. You are enough.

Always.

Chapter Three
PUT YOUR BIG GIRL PANTIES ON

After I found out I was going to be a single mom, everything changed. It hit me, I had someone who was going to depend on me for everything. Even though, I wanted to be the best version of myself, the truth was... I didn't even know who I was yet. I didn't know what I wanted to be. I had no direction. Just a baby on the way and a whole lot of pressure on my shoulders. I started working nights as a waitress at this local club. It wasn't glamorous, but it paid my bills. I was supposed to get off at midnight, but that's when the real money started coming in. So I stayed every night, until closing. Then I would go home, barely sleep, and somehow still try to make it to school by 6 a.m. Eventually, I couldn't keep up. I started skipping school just to get some rest. I would go to my sister's house, crash on her couch, and sleep like I hadn't slept in weeks. I was exhausted—physically, mentally, and emotionally. But I still showed up for the three classes I had to pass to graduate. That was my goal to just get those credits, just finish!

I was growing up fast, too fast! But somewhere in the middle of all that chaos—between the late nights, the early mornings, the swollen feet, and the silent tears I started becoming a woman. Not because I wanted to, but because I *had* to. There was this one teacher, I will never forget her. Something about her classroom, I could never stay awake in her class and it wasn't because I didn't care. Her class was right after lunch, and by the time I sat down in that seat, my eyes would get so heavy, it was like clockwork. I don't know if it was the food, the lights, or just the fact that I was *exhausted*. She taught algebra and I needed that class to graduate. I did pull her to the side and say, "Look, I'm not being disrespectful. I'm trying. I'm really trying." But how do you explain to a teacher that you've been up all night working a job, then going home to take care of a baby, then waking up and showing up to school trying to hold yourself together? I was only 17, still a teenager: but already doing what grown-ass women have to do. Unfortunately, she didn't care. Her energy toward me was cold. She was real nonchalant. She looked me dead in my face and said, "If I give you slack because you have a child, then I would have to give everyone else slack, too." I get it, maybe. But damn! I wasn't asking for a handout, I was asking for grace. Still, she said if I passed the final exam, I could graduate. So I studied like crazy, late nights after feeding my baby and early mornings before school. I thought I passed that exam. I really thought I did it! I thought I made it, but when it got close to graduation, things got weird. Time was ticking, and I still hadn't received confirmation that I was cleared to walk. I started getting that sinking feeling in my stomach like something was off. Then it hit me like a brick, I was failing her class by **one damn point.** I had 69 points. One point away from passing. One point was keeping me from walking across that stage in front of my family, my baby, everyone who believed in me. She refused to give it to me. I begged. I cried and I explained again, I wasn't just some student who was slacking off. I told her, "I'm working nights, raising a whole child, still showing up every morning trying to finish this damn thing." However, she stood on her decision, no mercy, no extra credit and no 70%. Just a 69. I had to sit there and watch people I sat next to all year walk across that stage while I sat in the stands with a diploma I couldn't claim, because of *one point*. That moment hurt, deeply. It also lit something in me, because life doesn't always give you extra points. Sometimes people will close a door right in your face, not knowing how hard you fought just to get to the door. In spite of it all, I kept going, because I had a baby watching me and I couldn't fold. I was tired. I was disappointed. But I was becoming a woman who knew how to get back up even after people tried to keep me down.

So yeah, I ended up failing 12th grade. Honestly, it was one of the lowest points of my life. I had to go to summer school, which already felt like punishment, and on top of that, I was working nights just to help out at home. So imagine this: I would get off work super late, barely sleep, and then drag myself to summer school in the morning. That summer was weird. They made summer school online, and we didn't even have real teachers, just these teacher assistants. It felt like they didn't care if we passed or not. I remember walking into class, barely able to keep my eyes open. I was so exhausted all the time, and I didn't even know I was dealing with an illness back then. I just thought I was lazy or something. But I had *zero* energy. Then there was this one teacher assistant. I swear, she was like an angel or something. I can't remember her name or even her face clearly now, but I'll never forget how she made me feel. She saw right through everything. She told me she thought the whole setup was unfair, like they were setting the seniors up to fail. Instead of just watching us struggle, she actually helped.

She started helping everyone with their work, but with me... it was different. We had these deep talks, and she really listened. She understood what I was going through. Then, one day, she just told me to rest. Like actually, she allowed me lay my head down and sleep. While I was out cold, she did my assignments, all of them. I know that sounds wild, but I think she knew I needed more than just academic help; I needed someone to believe in me and she did. I don't know where I would be if she had not stepped in that summer.

Graduating high school was supposed to be a big deal. Like, a huge milestone. But for me, it honestly just felt like something that was getting in the way. I didn't feel celebrated. I was already used to that, being overlooked I mean. I was actually excited about the prom. I thought maybe that would be my moment. I had an older boyfriend who was too old to go to a prom. I bought an $80.00 dress from Dillard's, it wasn't designer or anything, but it made me feel pretty. I paid to get my hair done, went to the eye doctor all by myself, and even bought my first pair of contacts. I wanted to feel like someone that night. I drove myself to the prom with one of my single girlfriends. No date, no big entrance, no pictures. Not even one. A night that should have been magical ended up being something I did completely on my own. Yeah, it hurts. Then graduation came and went. Instead of feeling proud or excited, I just felt… pressure. Like, "Okay, now what?" I didn't know what I wanted to be, but I knew I had to be somebody. Mom was kind of doing her own thing. My dad wasn't around. So I made a decision, I enrolled myself into the local community college. No help, no guidance. Just me. I remember coming home and telling everyone, thinking maybe *this* would be the moment they would be proud. But it was like… nothing, just another day. Don't get me wrong, my mom is a good woman; but at the time, she was dealing with a lot. Her husband couldn't keep a job, and I had a baby, so that meant one more mouth to feed. It felt like I was growing up in fast-forward, doing all the "big" things alone. I guess that's what made me stronger.

One day, my mom came to me with this look in her eyes like, not angry or sad exactly, but just different, tired. She said, "August 26th and 27th , we have to be out of this house." Just like that. No buildup, no warning. We were getting evicted, again! I heard her, but I didn't *really* hear her, you know? It went in one ear and out the other. I didn't pack. I didn't ask questions. I didn't do *anything*. I was 17 years old, and yeah, people were treating me like I was grown; but inside, I was still just a kid trying to figure it all out. So August 26th or 27th rolls around, and I go to work like it's just another night. I got off around 3 a.m., tired and ready to crash. I walk into the house and everything was packed. Like, *everything*. Boxes stacked, furniture moved, like the whole place was ready to disappear. I just stood there, frozen. Even though she told me, I was still shocked. It was like my brain had blocked it out, like if I didn't think about it, it would not have been real. I looked at my mom, completely confused, and asked, "Where are we going?" She was crouched down, taping up another box, and she looked up at me with this exhausted face like she hadn't slept in days and all she said was, "See if your sister has room for you." That was it, no plan. I just had to figure it out. I just stood there, speechless. My heart dropped. Like, literally sank into my stomach. I didn't even know what to say or feel. That's when it hit me, I was *homeless*. No room, no plan, no one asking me what I needed or how I felt. Just... figure it out. I was 17 years old, still a kid in so many ways. In that moment, I realized I didn't have a place to call mines, anymore. Everything I owned was in boxes. I didn't pack, and the only direction I got was to go and see if someone else had space for me. It was like the world just kept moving, and I was standing still, trying to catch up.

Dear 17 years old, Domonique,

I know right now it feels like the world has forgotten you. Like you're invisible, carrying more than anyone your age should ever have to carry. But I need you to know—this moment does not define you. It's just a chapter, not the whole story.

You are not weak for feeling tired. You are not a failure because life got hard. You are surviving something that would break many, and you're doing it with strength you don't even realize you have, yet.

You will learn how to build a life from the ground up. You will find your voice, your purpose, and your peace. One day, you'll look back and be proud—not just because you made it, but because you never gave up, even when no one was clapping for you.

So cry, if you need to and rest when you can. But don't stop. You are worthy of love, of stability, and of joy. You are going to be so much more than this moment. Keep going. You're not alone—even when it feels like it.

Chapter Four
YOU GROWN NOW

Imagine being seventeen, with an 11th month-old baby on your hip, and nowhere to go, homeless. The worst part is, your pride won't let you ask for help; because you don't want to be a burden. That was me. All I had to my name was a $730 check from financial aid and some tips I made waitressing that night. My mom had told me to see if my sister had room for me, but I never called, I couldn't. My sister was already doing everything on her own, raising her kids, holding it down. I didn't want to be one more thing she had to carry. So me and this guy friend of mines drove around the city, looking for a hotel. We went to four different places, and I kept thinking about safety, coming in late at night with a baby, just the two of us. Finally, we found this Extended Stay on Kirby. It was brand new $300 a week, or $50 a night if I couldn't swing the full week. That's where I landed.

I had just started college. I was paying my auntie to watch my baby while I went to class. I would leave school, pick up my baby, try to spend a little time with him, then drop him back off so I could go to work. After my shift, I would pick him up again in the middle of the night and head back to the hotel. Every single day, it was very exhausting. I was running on fumes, but I kept going. Then my 18th birthday started creeping up. My sister who always had a way of showing up when it mattered, suggested that I start looking for an apartment. I didn't even know where to begin, but she helped me.

She guided me through it, looking at places, thinking about safety, making sure I would be somewhere decent. That was the beginning of something new. I didn't have it all figured out, but I was learning. I was growing. I was surviving.

There was a moment, just a small window when my son's father offered to keep our baby while I got on my feet. For a second, I thought maybe things were turning around. Unfortunately, that only lasted a week. One day, my professor didn't show up to class, so I decided to use that time to go see my son before work. I just wanted to sit with him, hold him, feel like a mom again for a little while. We played, laughed, and for a moment, it felt like we were a family. However, time doesn't stop, and I had to leave for work. I knew he was going to cry when he saw me leave, he always did. So I asked his dad to pick him up so I could sneak out. Truth is, leaving him every time just about *killed* me. Let's be real, I was living in a hotel, trying to make the best decision I could with what I had. As I was slipping out the door, my baby saw me. His little face crumpled, and he started crying. That's when I saw his dad reach for a switch, what country folks call a thin stick from a tree used for a whooping. My heart dropped. I *snapped*. He wasn't even one years old, yet. He didn't understand why I was leaving. He just wanted his mama. I went off. I was furious, scared, heartbroken, and feeling all of it; but I still had to leave. I had to go to work. I needed those tips to pay for the hotel. I cried the whole way there, not because I thought his dad would hurt him, I knew he wouldn't. We were just two dumb teenagers trying to figure out life and parenthood at the same time. But still, it broke me. That next morning, I didn't hesitate. I went and picked up my baby. I didn't care what it took, I just knew he needed to be with me.

The day had finally come, my 18th birthday. It was a Friday, and I only had one morning class, but you better believe I showed up like it was a red carpet event. I had on all white with gold accessories, and shorts? Yeah, those shorts made my booty pop just right. I strutted into class like, *"Can't nobody tell me nothin'—I'm grown now!"* But I wasn't just dressed up for the birthday vibes, I had business to handle. I had already decided on the apartment I wanted, and I had called ahead to make sure I had everything I needed to apply. My money orders were ready, and even though I didn't know what to expect, I was hopeful. I walked into that leasing office by myself, confident. Before the lady could even ask for anything, I laid it all out on her desk, my ID, pay stubs, money orders, everything. I was prepared. She looked at me and said, "We'll give you a call." I left there not knowing what was next. I didn't even make it a full block away when my phone rang. It was the leasing office. "You're approved for the apartment!" I swear, it felt like a thousand pounds had been lifted off my shoulders. I wanted to cry, but the tears wouldn't come. I just kept whispering, "Thank you, Jesus! Thank you, Jesus!" I had only been homeless for a few weeks, but in that moment, I felt something shift. I felt *independent*. I felt like I had something to prove and I was proving it. I was so proud of myself. That day, I knew I could do *anything*, because I was grown now!

Domonique,

"You didn't just survive—you rose. You were scared, tired, and unsure, but you never stopped moving. You made choices with a heart full of love and a mind full of determination. You protected your baby, you showed up for work, for school, for life, even when no one showed up for you.

You didn't wait for someone to save you. You became your own rescue. I'm so proud of you for not giving up. For crying when you needed to, but still getting up the next day.

For choosing dignity over pity. For proving that even in the darkest moments, you were still worthy of light.
You are strong. You are capable. You are enough.
Everything you went through, built the woman you are today!

Chapter Five
KARMA'S A BITCH

I like to think I was raised in a pretty traditional home. My mom was an Evangelist, my stepdad a Preacher. We were in church every Sunday, all day Sunday. I was what they called a "quartet baby," raised on the gospel, structure, and knowing right from wrong. When I turned 18, I had this new "I'm grown now" energy. I was working at a local club where the men had to be 25 and up just to get in. Being around that scene, I started to build this "bad chick" confidence. I started dating older men. One of them was the president of a bike club and he loved to show out for me, I loved the attention. He would have new recruits running to do things for me just to flex his power. I was 18 years old and he was 27 years old. I thought I was winning, but I wasn't. I was just a young trophy to him. He would say he was coming and never showed up. I'd call him, but no answer. When he finally did responded, it was always some dramatic excuse. Life or death, every time. I started to see through it. My sister's boyfriend worked as a bouncer at the club, and one of his best friends worked with him on weekends. He used to flirt with me, but my sister had made it *very* clear, I was off limits.

Then one night, my biker boyfriend stood me up, again. This time, I was *done*. I was mad, hurt, and tired of feeling like I didn't matter. That night, my sister's boyfriend's friend was looking real good. So with all the confidence I had in me, I looked at him and said, "Are you taking me to breakfast tonight?"

He stuttered, caught completely off guard then he said, "Well, well… yelp!" That was the moment. The shift. The secret I kept for a long time. Not because I was ashamed, but because it was the first time I realized I was making choices—not always the right ones—but they were *mine*. I was learning, growing, and figuring out who I was outside of the church girl, the "quartet baby," the preacher's kid.

My affair started like a secret I never meant to keep, but I couldn't let go of it. Let me tell you, this man was *fine*. Six feet tall, chocolate brown, 230 pounds of solid confidence. Broad shoulders that looked like they were built just to hold me. He had a tattoo across his right cheek that read "M-O-M-M-A", he was a little street, and little sweet. He had just enough thug in him to make you feel protected, but when he opened his mouth, all knew he was smart. He handled business. He had presence, but he was married and I knew it. He knew it. However, in that moment of my life, I didn't care. I wasn't thinking about his wife, or my worth, or the consequences. I was thinking about *me*. I only let it happen, because the man I really wanted had chosen to be somewhere else. Remember, I was grown now, right? I could do whatever I wanted!

So for about a year, we snuck around. He had his wife. I still had my biker boyfriend who kept disappointing me. My son's grandmother started getting my baby on the weekends, and after the club closed, we'd meet at my apartment. No one knew. We played our roles. I knew my place. He knew his, but then he started catching feelings.

He was getting reckless. He would stay too long. The sun started catching us, and his wife, she started noticing. His insecurities started showing. I broke up with the biker boyfriend, thinking maybe this was it, maybe we were about to be real. His wife moved out and took their sons. Now, all he wanted was *me*. But before we could even show the world what we had been hiding for a year; I had to tell my sister, first. I had kept this huge secret from her, and when I finally told her, she was *pissed*. She didn't approve of our relationship, at all. I was at that point in my life, where I felt grown. I was going to do what I wanted, whether people liked it or not. Still, her opinion meant the most to me, so it hurt knowing she didn't support it. I told myself—*she can accept it or not, I'm doing me!*

He was always around. His charm, his humor, it always pulled people in. He was the life of the party, the one who always brought the liquor, the one everyone gravitated toward, and me, I was 19 years old. He was 37 years old. What started as an affair turned into something that felt, deeper. It started to feel like a father-daughter dynamic in some ways. He taught me how to open my first bank account. How to manage bills. How to carry myself with confidence and strength. He even coached me on how to check people when they got out of line and sometimes even using his own cousins to test me. He was the first person I thought I fell in love with. As our relationship grew, so did his insecurities. His paranoia. He had this way of checking other men, if they looked at me too long, or talked to me too much. He wasn't rude, he was smooth with it. He would joke, but everyone knew he meant it and somehow, people respected it. They respected him. Now that I look back, it reminds me of how my dad was with women. That same energy. That same sense of control, wrapped in charm. He made you feel like you were a big deal. Like it was a *privilege* for people to even speak to you and for a while, I believed it.

So here we are, three years deep into this relationship, and it had gone way passed toxic. I remember nights where I was on the floor, crying, literally begging God to take the feelings away. He had my mind so twisted, I couldn't see past him. I was stuck in something that felt like love, but looked nothing like it. It was New Year's Eve. We weren't even speaking. I don't remember what the argument was about, but I remember the silence. I sent him a sarcastic text: *"So we're going into the new year not speaking to each other?"* I don't even remember if he replied. I went to work like usual, waitressing at the club. It was packed, of course, because it was New Year's. A little after midnight, my phone started blowing up. Back-to-back calls from him, like he forgot I was working. I finally stepped away for a second to answer. I told him I would come by after my shift. What I didn't mention was that he was from East St. Louis, and for the holiday, all his people were in town. He was throwing a party at his place, just two minutes from the club. When I pulled up, cars were lined down the street. But what caught my eye was this white Cherokee Jeep parked outside. It looked *just* like mines, identical. I walked in, and the first person I saw was my sister's boyfriend, he was drunk and talking to himself like he was having a full-blown conversation. I stepped over people who were passed out on the floor. Then I made my way to the couch and there he was, my man. He was *sleep*. After all that drama, all those calls, all that silence. I couldn't believe he was just laid out on the couch like nothing happened.

I sat on the edge of the couch and gently woke him up. When he opened his eyes, he embraced me like he was genuinely happy to see me. I gave him a big hug back. The house was packed with people everywhere so I told him I would be right back, just wanted to go speak to everyone. I ended up in a room talking to one of his cousin's girlfriends, just catching up. Then he walked in and his whole vibe had changed. He stood in the doorway with this hard, cold look on his face and said, *"Get out."* I was stunned. Two minutes ago, he was hugging me like I was the only person in the world. Now I was being kicked out like I didn't belong. I looked at the girl and said, "You see what I have to deal with?" Embarrassed, confused, I started walking down the hallway. That's when I ran into my cousin, who was also friends with him, and realized he was there to get bullets from him for a gun. I didn't know what was going on, but I left. On the drive home, I called my sister. She asked if her boyfriend was still there. I told her yeah, and that he was drunk. Then I heard noise in the background and asked where she was going. That's when she told me, everyone was headed to our little cousin's house. Her boyfriend had tried to put his hands on her, and when that didn't work, he called a group of girls to come jump her. What the fuck is going on? Is it a full moon? My family wasn't going for that. Suddenly, everything made sense. The reason why my cousin was getting bullets, and why the energy in that house felt off. My guy probably knew what was going on the whole time. I turned on my emergency lights and hit the highway. We all gathered at my cousin's house. The police came, and we watched him packed up all his stuff. Because yeah, he had to go!

So finally, I'm heading home. I thought let me, give my boyfriend a call to check-in. I was talking to him all the way home. Again, I am getting this off feeling and he's talking to me very calmly, as if he's laying in the bed, or as if he didn't just make me leave his house. I pulled up at my now duplex and I seen that same white identical white Cherokee Jeep sitting right across the street from my house and when I noticed it I asked him "Is this you sitting in this truck?" The entire way home I had be talking to him, and he was sitting outside my house. He began to mumble, "I caught you!" I said, "What did you catch?" "I caught, I caught you coming from the nigga's house!" I literally went from 1-100, hollering in the phone, probably to the point where you could not understand anything that I was saying. I knew I hadn't done anything wrong. Remember, I'm young and I just react. I went into my house with him still sitting in the car and I'm still hollering as I'm putting my things down. He finally hangs up the phone and comes to the door, and for the first time in three years of this relationship, I felt like I should not open the door. I opened it anyways, and he walked right passed me and went into my hall bathroom which was jack and jill to my master's bedroom and he began to stand at the toilet and pee. As he stood at the toilet, I was standing next to him saying, "How could you even think I was with another man when my cousin came over to get bullets from you, because of my cousin?" He finished using the bathroom and look at me with a demon look. There was something different in his eyes and he only said, very calmly "You bitch, you hoe, you slut." I stared right back at him and told him, "Like you got me fuck up, get out my house!" He repeated "Get out yo house?" I said, "Yeah, get the fuck out of my house!" As he walked towards me getting in my face. I agreed, "Yelp, get yo ass out my house!" With my head high looking him straight in his eyes, with no fear. What felt like with all his might, he balled up his fist and punched me right in my face. Shocked from the hit, I couldn't even fight back. I ran into my bedroom, and in straight panic mode, standing in my bed. I tried to call my sister; it seemed like everything was happening so fast. He snatched the phone out of my hand and threw it into the wall and punches me, again. Where I fell into the bed, and at this point all I knew to do, was to fight back. He was now on top of me, just punching me. I was then fighting back, what felt like I was fighting for dear life and we constantly fought until we rolled off the bed. As he punched me, I punched back. But hell, I was being punched by a man; so I damn near wanted to give up after every punch. My room was always set up the exact same way as it is now. My bed was in the middle and my

50

night stands on each side of the bed with matching lamps. As we rolled on the side of bed, still fighting each other he landed on top of me. I managed to grabbed the lamp and hit him on top of the head with the lamp which psst him off even more. Remember, I told you he had a thug side to him and he was a guy who always carried a 9 mm on the side of his hip. He actually was the first person who taught me how to shoot a gun. So now he was on top of me, and I hit him over the head with a lamp. I really think I was starting to get the best of him, so he reached for his gun. Now, he was on top of me and I was on the floor and I was fighting for dear life with this gun in my face! Struggling and trying to make sure the gun didn't go off, I tried to distract him. The only thing I could think of was my son, and that this was the way it was about to end. I cried out, "Think of Kion!" Still tussling with this gun in my face, he yelled out, "Fuck Kion!" I was fighting so hard so that gun wouldn't go off in my face, that I tired him out. I couldn't give up, He stopped fighting me. He was super exhausted breathing hard. Both of us, were breathing hard. He grabbed me by my hair with his left hand and with the right hand he had the gun pointed in my face. He yelled at me telling me, "Get up!" While still holding me by my hair, he grabbed me and threw me across the bed, never letting my hair go and never dropping the gun! Now, he has me laying vertically over the bed, holding my hair and he takes the gun and start rubbing my hair with the gun. Whispering, "I want to talk," as he was trying to catch his breath.

While he is trying to catch his breath, in the silence, I started praying very loudly, "God forgive me for my sins, God take care of my baby. God, I'm sorry!" He yelled, "Shut up bitch!" I ignored him and I continued to pray out loud. I was repenting right there, it was clear I wasn't getting out of this situation. It seemed like a demon came over him and he yelled even louder, "Shut up bitch!" He took the gun and pushed it in my temple, and I got quiet. I felt like my entire body was shaking, but something in me would not allow me to show him my weakness. All I kept thinking about was my son and how heartbroken I was feeling; because I was looking at a man who I thought I loved. So he told me he just wanted to talk and he was going to let me up. He never took the gun away from pointing at me. I sat up at the left side of the end of my bed, and he moved up to the left side of the head board of the bed, still pointing the gun at me. I said, "What do you want to talk about?" Looking him straight in the face! He began to start asking me questions, about every time that he thought I may have cheated on him and it seems like some stuff I was going to take to my grave. Because I was not about to psst him off, no more than he was already. I remember one question that he felt like I didn't answer truthfully, and he took the gun and hit me in the face with it, and he took the pillow and put it over my face; as if he was going to shoot through the pillow. At that point, I was done answering questions and I began to just pray out loudly, "God, forgive me of my sins. God, please take care of my baby. God, I'm sorry!"

It's crazy to say, but I had actually gave up and I was making my peace with what I thought was about to happen. I began to see, he was pistol playing with me. He started to say that his lips were chapped and that he needed his chapstick. So he walked me to the bathroom, where the fight started with the gun in my back. I realized I had done fought him out of two shirts. He moved his two shirts and found his chapstick on the floor and he asked me, with the gun still pointed at me, to put the chapstick on his lips. Everything within me wanted to hit him in his mouth. Me, being scared started to grow into anger, and anger started growing into "Fucking psst off!" We made it back to the bed and I was done talking. He started rambling on, talking about how we had made love in this bed so many times, still waving the gun in his hand. I was just looking at him with disgust and the meanest mean mug. This shit was beginning to be something straight out of a fucking lifetime movie; to the point I cut him off in mid sentence and I said, "Just do it." He looked at me in shock and said, "Do what?" I said, "Just shoot me! Let's get this shit over with. I'm not answering any more questions and I'm okay with what's about to happen." He just stared at me with no words and eyes became very droopy, as if he was falling asleep. The gun began to become very limped in his hand and it seems like we just sat there in silence. He began to fall asleep and I thought to myself, "I know you are fucking lying, how could he just fall asleep? But Baby you can't tell me what my God won't do. In that movement, I

53

wasn't scared. I had made my peace with God and the devil didn't scare me. I didn't move and I never took my eyes off of him. The gun fell out of his hand from him being asleep and he was now laid in the bed. I moved from the end of the bed to sitting on the night stand next to him, where the gun was at arms reach. I was in complete shock that he was asleep. So now I started thinking, I watched him go into a deep sleep where he rolls and he rolls and then he falls off the bed. He is now laying on the floor on his back with his arms stretched out and I still feel like I am being tested! The gun was laying right there with me, now. I started thinking one shot to the chest, and I'm out of here. Then I started thinking about my baby. Jail, never never crossed my mind. See, he had told me some things he had done in the past, and I kept thinking no matter what he just done to me, if I kill him I start a war with his folks and my family. All that I could think of, was that my baby would be the first to go. So I never touched the gun. I walked to the bathroom and began to use the bathroom. Just trying to make some type of noise, to see if he would move. Still watching through the mirrors of my Jack-n-Jill bathroom, I thought to myself where are my keys? I started moving the shirts that I had fought him out of, and found my keys on the floor. I grabbed them whole, just enough for them not to make any noise and I ran out of the door. As I ran out of door, I realized my door had been opened the entire time, while I had been in there fighting for my life. I could have been in my house dead, and no one would have ever known. As I drove, all I could think of me and my sister are so close, she must have known something was going on with me. I drove straight to her house, beating on her door. When she opened it, I fell in her arms crying, "He tried to kill me!" God showed me early: you will never find true happiness by causing someone else pain. But, I didn't understand that back then. I didn't realize I was walking in my father's footsteps doing whatever it took to feel good in the moment, even if it meant hurting others. His wife didn't deserve the pain I helped caused her. I don't know if she will ever read this, but if she does... *I apologize!* Truly!

They say, "You can't miss what you never had." That's a lie! I didn't know how much I needed a man to tell me I was beautiful, that I mattered. That should have been my father's job. I didn't know, I would have to go through heartbreak and chaos just to find the strength and wisdom that I was missing, but I did. I had to learn the hard way. Now I know, *karma is real*! She doesn't miss! I also know this: I'm not that girl, anymore! I have grown. I have healed. I can say, I am still healing. I have learned to forgive myself, to take accountability, and to move forward with grace. Because the woman I am now, she's not perfect, but she's powerful! Finally, she's free!

Men who have daughters, you must remember this:

A daughter's first love is always her father. Whether you're present or absent, your impact echoes through her life. Many women grow up and unknowingly fall in love with men who mirror our fathers, sometimes in the best ways, but often in the ways that hurt the most. I wasn't raised by my father, but I was still his blood. I carried his genes, his ways, and unknowingly, some of his wounds. The man I loved reminded me so much of my father, and I didn't even realize how much I was missing that male role in my life, until it was too late. This wasn't the only abuse I endured, but it was the most significant. It broke something in me—but it also woke something up in me.
God got me through.
When you know better, you do better.
To the woman I was: I see you.
To the woman I am now: I'm proud of you.
To the fathers out there: Be the man you want your daughter to believe in.

Chapter Six
NEVER SAW IT COMING

Whew... let me tell you something—three days of labor pains *without* an epidural will have you begging the doctor for birth control right then and there. No lie! As soon as I hit nine months pregnant, it was like my doctor already had a calendar marked, he was scheduling my induction before I could even breathe. But my baby? Oh, he had his *own* plans. From day one, my body was playing games, it wouldn't dilate past one centimeter. Just one. So there I was, going through a full day of what felt like pointless, agonizing contractions. No progress. Just pain. They finally let me rest that night, only to start the whole thing up again the next morning. And baby, day two? It was *worse* than the first. Still, only two centimeters. I was exhausted, starving, thirsty, and mad at the world, especially at my mama. She was the only one who could sign off on the epidural since I was just sixteen and she held off. She was right there by my side, coaching me, doing what mamas do, trying to keep me strong. She even cracked a joke, saying, "You'll think twice about having another one after this." I gave her a side eye, but she wasn't wrong. Because I was so young and pregnant, she had put me in these parenting classes. Honestly, I was terrified, scared of the epidural needle. Scared of a C-section. Scared of *everything*. After two full days of pain and no real progress, the doctors gave me a choice: either have a C-section or go home without a baby. I chose to go home. I was heartbroken, and defeated. I went home crying, cramping, and feeling like the world had swallowed me up whole. But two days later, on his own time my little superstar came into this world, just four days before my 17th birthday. And let me tell you... he gave me a reason to keep going. He gave me purpose. I didn't know it then, but everything changed when I held him for the first time. A year later, here I am finally settling into my new apartment, living my best life. Balancing being a mom, being a full-grown adult. Life was starting to feel stable, until it shifted. My mom had gotten a little sick nothing too serious, thank God. It gave me the perfect excuse to be babied for once. So I went over to her place and climbed into bed with her, just to keep her company. I mean, I was still technically a teenager, so I needed that comfort too. Then her phone rang. It was a call from *my* doctor's office. They'd apparently been trying to get in touch with me. Now, let me give you a little backstory, I had just found out that my motorcycle-riding boyfriend had been cheating on me, and I was *done*. I ended the relationship and, in true "Matthews" fashion, changed my number. So yeah, the doctor's office couldn't reach me. The nurse on the phone sounded completely panicked. Like, **seriously** panicked. She told me I needed to stop what I was doing and get to the nearest hospital *immediately* to give blood, they were prepping me for emergency surgery. Wait, what? Ma'am, I need more information before I just run into a hospital! At the time, I had so much going on, college classes, single motherhood, just moved into my new apartment after living out of a hotel for a bit. Honestly, I kept putting off my annual check-up. It got so bad my doctor had literally threatened not to refill my birth control prescription unless I came in. Life was moving fast and I just kept pushing it aside. Turns out, my pap smear had come back *abnormal*. I remember sitting there, frozen, my mind racing. What did that even mean? I had a million questions. The nurse, "Domonique!" was trying so hard to keep me calm. "Let's just take it one step at a time," she said gently, as she scheduled me for a next-day appointment. So I went. Nervous as hell, with my mom by my side, holding my hand like I was still her baby. That's when I heard the words no 18-year-old expects to hear: "You have cervical cancer."

By the grace of God, the surgery went well. I made it through. In just a few short months, I was in recovery and then, remission. I was so relieved. I thought I was in the clear. I could finally say it: *I survived cancer.*

Fast forward two years later, I woke up one morning in the worst pain I'd ever felt. I don't mean just a headache I mean my entire body was aching. My gums were swollen, like I had the worst toothache imaginable. I looked at my arms, and they were covered in these strange patches, I thought they were ringworms and I was itching. Oh my God, I itched like there were bugs crawling all over my body. I was alone in my apartment, crying, scared, and confused. I kept thinking, *Is this some kind of side effect from the cancer?* I didn't know what was happening to me. I just knew something was seriously wrong. My mouth hurt so bad, I couldn't even think straight. So I pulled myself together as best I could and drove to the nearest dentist office. Tears in my eyes, trying to explain the pain, barely able to keep it together while filling out the paperwork. That's when they told me I had aged out of my mom's dental insurance. There was nothing they could do for me. I sat there in the waiting room with my black hoodie pulled over my head, trying to hide how defeated I felt. I was hurting so bad the tears just kept falling. I looked up and told the assistant, "I had cancer. I don't know what's going on with me now, but something is not right." She looked at me with so much compassion. A black woman maybe a mother, maybe someone who had been through something herself, she didn't say much. She just placed her hands on me and started to pray. Right there in the middle of the office and in that moment, I swear God sent me comfort through her. Because, I was lost and I was tired. I didn't know what to do. Eventually, I got in to see my doctor and that's when I learned I had already tested positive for Lupus. Just like that my life changed, again. I was given some pain meds, a few vouchers, and sent home to figure out this whole new reality. Another diagnosis. Another fight. Once again, I had to learn how to live all over, again.

At this point, I honestly can't even remember the last time I spoke to my father. To be real with you, I didn't care to, I was grown now. What could a father do for me at this point? All my life, everything I ever heard about him sounded like something straight out of a horror story. Nothing good. Just pain, disappointment, and absence. Then one day, while I was at work, in walks this man, *my* father. He was bold as ever, like he owned the place, and with him he had a yellow, big-boned woman on his arm like he was strolling into a concert, not a bar. My older sister, who just so happened to be my manager at the time —was *pissed*. I mean, *fuming*. I just froze. I could feel butterflies in my stomach, but not the good kind, it was more like a storm. I watched my sister, and it was like her entire childhood hit her all at once. You could see it in her eyes. I had no words. Here was this man, who was pretty much a stranger to me, walking in and changing the whole energy in the room like it was nothing. He didn't care. He acted like nobody's feelings mattered. He was just there, loud and nonchalant, like, *"Yeah, I'm him and?"* He didn't even flinch that his presence had upset anybody. As for me, I followed my sister's lead; if she was mad, then I was mad too! Period.

But here's the crazy part: my daddy had this cocky attitude about him like, "If you don't like me, cool. I'll give you a reason not to." Somewhere deep down, I saw myself in that. I was so much like my daddy, and I didn't even know it. After that, he started showing up almost every night after his show. Every time, he brought a different woman, but they all looked like cousins— yellow, big-boned, flashy. Like he had a type and wasn't shy about it. Still, I never said a word to him. I never looked his way. I wouldn't even acknowledge he was there. But, you know what I'd heard? I heard him telling people, *"That's my daughter right there!"* Saying it, like he was proud. Proud of a daughter who wouldn't even speak to him and that messed with me in a way I wasn't ready to admit.

So one night, my Daddy came into the bar and of course, with a woman. But this time, she wasn't like the others. Nah, she was different. She was brown-skinned, elegant and she had that jazzy, old-school vibe, like she stepped out of a Billie Holiday's record. Her voice, whew was soft and smoky, like a blues singer that's lived a little. She didn't look like the usual light-skinned, big-boned women, he always came in with. She had presence and soul. Now me, I played it cool like always. Pretending not to notice him, like he didn't exist. The truth is, I was watching everything. I mean that was my father. The crazy part is, I didn't really know a thing about him. As I walked passed their table, I heard him again: *"That's my daughter, right there."* Same line, same pride, and something in me softened. I stopped, looked up, and smiled just enough. *"What y'all getting?"* I asked, calmly like it was just business. No emotion, just customer service. I wasn't trying to have a heart-to-heart, I was trying to get through the shift. He kept up the show, introducing himself to her like *Daddy Dearest*, like we was this happy little family. When they finished, he tipped me a hundred dollars, casually like it was nothing. Then they left. A week went by, out of nowhere, I got a call. It's was *her* that brown-skinned jazz lady. At first, I didn't even recognize the voice. Once I did, I thought, *"Oh, we bold now, huh?"* She was sweet, though. Real gentle with her words. She told me my Daddy wanted to talk to me, alone. Just him and me. I was like, *"Talk to me for what?"* Still holding on to all my attitude, and all my resentment; but she didn't give up. She said, "Just come over. I'll cook your favorite food." I couldn't help but smile. I said, "Neck bones?" She laughed and said, "If you come talk to your Daddy, I'll make you the best neck bones you ever had in your life." Next thing I know, I'm pulling up to her house, nervous as hell. Stubborn as I was, something in me needed that moment. Soon as I walked in, that smell hit me, whew. Seasoned *soul* food. My inner fat girl was ready, okay! I'm talking neck bones, cornbread, something simmering on the stove. It smelled like love and struggle all in one. She led me to what I guess was the den and there he was, my daddy! Sitting there like he had been waiting on me his whole life. He was a man of mystery, someone I barely knew, yet somehow, that day he felt familiar. He sat across from me, looking comfortable. Like he had just come out of something important. Slacks on, like he'd worn a suit earlier, but now dressed down in a plain white tank top. Big rings on both hands, and this huge, expensive-looking watch that caught the light every time he moved. I sat there, emotionless. I didn't say much. I just listened. He had just been diagnosed with diabetes, and I could tell it scared him. Maybe that's what brought him to me. Facing his mortality, trying to make sense of the past. He started talking about where things went wrong between him and my mom. He fumbled through it, awkward and unsure, but then his voice cracked and he started crying. Like really crying, he begged for my forgiveness. Said he knew he hadn't been there that he wanted to fix things whatever that looked like. As much as I tried to stay cold, tried to stay silent, it got to me. Because part of me had waited to hear those words my whole life. I had always heard the stories of how my mom, like so many black women, had battled fibroids and struggled to carry a child. But somehow I made it through. I was the baby who made it. In that moment, I could see it in his eyes, he saw me as his miracle child. That day, I had my first real meal with my dad. I couldn't help but notice, we ate exactly the same. No vegetables in sight, sugar on *everything*. It was weirdly comforting. Now, at 21 years old, I finally had a dad.

Chapter Seven
DADDY'S GIRL

They say a girl is never too old to be a daddy's girl and I believe that with my whole heart. For me and my dad, it wasn't something we forced. It just happened naturally like something we both needed, even if we didn't know it at the time. It started with the little things. He began calling every day just to check in, talk about nothing, or everything. Those calls became our lifeline. He wasn't just my dad anymore. He became my friend. My homie, my safe place. We started meeting for lunch, just the two of us. At the time, he was still building his name in Memphis, doing his thing on the radio. He had this duplex downtown that he turned into a studio. It was raw, real, and full of energy. He'd have me swing by sometimes to pick up money, sometimes just to hang out. I would sit and watch him do his blues show, then transition into his talk show like a pro. One day, he was talking about relationships on air, and I couldn't help myself, I jumped in. I thought he was way off! We debated, laughed, and I stood my ground. I was only 21 or 22 years old, but I had something to say. He saw that and he respected it. That's when it really began. He handed me the headphones and said, "Come on, let's do this." Just like that, I was on the radio. I'll never forget how that felt. Not just because it was exciting, but because we were bonding, really bonding.

In the beginning, I think he used money to try and win me over. Maybe it was guilt. Maybe it was his way of making up for lost time, but over time, it wasn't about that anymore. We genuinely enjoyed each other's company. I was always trying to make him laugh, and I think for the first time, he started to see himself in me and I loved that. Because no matter how grown I get, I'll always be his little girl.

Domonique Michelle Matthews, that's how my dad would say my name, like it was a song only he knew the melody to and back then, I'd roll my eyes, a little embarrassed, but deep down, I loved it. I was his youngest, his baby. Even though he had kids before me, I was the first to really call him *"dad."* Truth is, he was just learning how to be one. Like me, he had been estranged from his older kids. So in a way, we were both starting fresh. Figuring it out together and even though our bond was new, it was real.

Remember his girlfriend at the time, wasn't his usual type. She was brown-skinned, jazzy, with a soulful voice that made you stop and listen. She got me a job at the dentist's office where she worked. I was juggling a lot; waitressing, bartending, finishing my bachelor's degree, and raising my baby as a single mom. Money was tight so I took the job, but it wasn't what I expected. I wasn't assisting the dentist, I was babysitting. Sometimes twenty kids at a time. Feeding them what felt like a thousand peanut butter sandwiches. It was a dentist office for low-income kids with state insurance. The women who worked there drove vans around neighborhoods, picking up kids for cleanings, hoping they'd find a cavity or two. Everyone had a quota, even the doctors, and me, I was just trying to survive. Every day, like clockwork Daddy's girlfriend would have his radio show playing loud and proud. Soon enough, the other women found out I was his daughter. At first, I didn't think much of it. I was always respectful, and always kind. Then came the tension, the side-eyes and the slick comments. I started to feel like "the help," not part of the team. I knew I was too smart for that job. However, I needed the money. I hadn't even met the owner yet. One day, someone said, *"The boss is on the way."* Suddenly, the whole place shifted. Women straightened up, fixed their hair, and checked their makeup. That's when I realized this wasn't just about work. There was a whole other game being played and I was watching it all unfold.

The day he walked in, you could feel the shift in the air. The Boss, he looked like old money. He was black, older, gray-headed, with that good hair and a smooth kind of swag that made a woman, pause. Handsome in that classic, grown-man way. The kind of man who didn't have to say much, because his presence said it all. The ladies, oh they flocked. Laughing a little too loud, fixing their hair, trying to catch his eye. He walked in like, *"Yeah, I own this place,"* and the thing is—he did. So I wasn't mad at it, and I didn't move. I wasn't impressed. Still, he noticed me, a new face. He walked over with that Billy Dee Williams charm, smooth and respectful, like I was some new tenderoni that he was curious about. He asked me questions, my name, how long I'd been there, what I did before, and if I was in school. I answered politely, but in my head I was thinking, *"Yeah, I'm in the wrong position."* Apparently, he thought the same. What I didn't know was that after our little chat, he went straight to the head manager. The next day, boom! I was promoted to front desk assistant with a pay raise. I was excited! Finally, a little recognition, a little light. The other ladies were not so much in agreement. Just when I thought I was moving up, I realized if I was leaving the babysitting gig, someone had to take my place. That's when the games began. The ladies had a trick up their sleeves. So boom they hit me with, "You'll train at the front desk in the morning, then babysit in the afternoon." "What?" I was piss. Like, how does that even make sense? Mind you, these ladies were pulling up with vans full of kids like a whole field trip every day. Suddenly, the office was "too busy" for me to be up front? Nah, I wasn't buying it. I overheard them arguing about who didn't want to train me. Like I was some burden and I couldn't understand where all the beef was coming from. I was respectful, I stayed in my lane, but why the tension? It was thick and I was getting sick of it.

My daily convos with my dad started turning into vent sessions. I'd call him just to let it out, how I was tired of the shade, the fake smiles, the way they tried to box me in. I was the oddball, no doubt; but I held my own. I gave them that look like, *"Don't play with me."* See, before this, I worked in a nightclub. Let's just say, fighting every weekend was starting to feel like cardio. So yeah, I thought about it, a lot; but I had too much to lose. Still, hearing what I was going through every day, started to get under my dad's skin. When my dad gets fired up he *says something.* Trust me, when he speaks, people listen. I needed a break. Mentally, emotionally because I was drained. So I took a day off from that dentist office circus. I just needed to breathe. Even on my day off, daddy's girlfriend had the radio on, like always and there he was my dad, live on air, doing what he does best. Only this time, it wasn't just music or talk. It was *personal.* He had a message and not just any message, a *warning.* He called out the owner of the dentist office by name on the radio. In that deep, commanding voice of his, he said: "You might want to play with someone else's child and not play with mines." Oh My God! The whole office was buzzing, phones were ringing and people were whispering. Shocked! They were shook and me, I was getting calls, too. Part of me was like, *"That's what they get!"* But another part of me, was stunned. Like, did that really just happen? When I went back to work, just like that I was fired. No explanation. No warning. Just gone. Oh, they messed up big time. I came back just to grab my things and they wouldn't even let me do that. That was it. Gloves off. I gave them what I'd been holding in for weeks: a good ol' **Matthews Cursing Out!** The kind that echoes in the walls and leaves folks blinking in silence and baby for the next two weeks, that dentist office was the topic on my dad's radio show. He opened up the phone lines, and whew people had stories. Folks were calling in left and right, spilling tea, sharing their own experiences. The city was eating it up. Memphis was tuned in and now, everybody knew who I was, Domonique. The one you don't mess with, because her daddy's coming, and low key: I loved it! My daddy was my protector, my security, and my hype man. He had me on a princess pedestal, and the city was watching. The drama kept unfolding insurance fraud, workplace affairs, it was like a soap opera on air. But then, I started to feel bad. People were losing their jobs. Not just the ones who came for me, but the ones who were cool with me, too. If you even looked like you supported me, the owner was letting you go, and that hurts. I never wanted to bring harm to anyone; but strangely, it backfired on him. Firing those folks only made the buzz louder. Now the co-workers had turned on him and they had *all* the tea. They wanted to fight back. They planned a day, *"We're going to the EEOC,"* they said. Filing complaints, and demanding lost wages. I thought it was a lot, but I couldn't disagree. These people had lost their jobs because of me. It turns out though, I was the only one with a real case, discrimination, and racial profiling. The office manager, the one who refused to train me, was Hispanic and just like that, the tables turned. They paid me a lump sum of money, quiet money, hush money. Basically, to shut my daddy up and let me tell you something, it worked. However, the city never forgot, and neither did I. This was just one of the many wild chapters I lived through with my daddy. Let me tell you something, *you couldn't tell me nothing about him.* All those horror stories I used to hear growing up, they started to fade. To me, those people just didn't understand him like I did. Because the man I knew, he was soft with me, honest and transparent. He was my hero. My superman and as his name grew bigger, so did his power in the city. My daddy was becoming that man, the one people loved to hate, but never dared to cross. He had a voice that could shake a room and a presence that demanded respect. As for me, I was his baby girl that meant I only had the best.

In my head, I was the only one he truly trusted. I had him wrapped around my finger, and I knew it. I was off-limits, untouchable. I started to get used to the looks, the whispers, the recognition, *"That's Domonique, his daughter,"* and I wore that title like a crown. People would boast about how crazy he was, how bold, and how unfiltered. I'd just smile, because I knew the man behind the mic. The one who'd go to war for me without blinking. As his popularity exploded, so did his ego. He leaned into the title of *"The Most Controversial Man in Town."* He pushed limits, stirred pots, and made sure everyone knew he wasn't here to play nice. As for me, I was right there, front row, watching my daddy become a legend.

I was *truly* a daddy's girl. No doubt about it. I loved my dad with everything in me. Let me tell you, *the ladies* loved my daddy, too. Now, being his daughter came with its fair share of embarrassment. I mean, imagine being a teenager and hearing grown women call your dad **"Thaddy Bear."** I thought it was the cheesiest, corniest thing ever. But my dad, he *loved* it. He wore that nickname like a badge of honor, literally. He wouldn't wear a suit unless it had "Thaddy Bear" embroidered somewhere on it. Then there were the panties. Yes, panties with his *face* on them. He sold them like hotcakes. I was mortified back then, but now? I laugh every time I think about it. That was my dad, an entrepreneur through and through. He was the brand,

71

loud, bold, and unforgettable. As for me, I was just like him, trying to find my own way. I started businesses, chased ideas, and every time, my dad was right there. He gave me office space, bought up my products like I was the next big thing, and blasted free advertising to all his fans. He believed in me, even when I didn't fully believe in myself.

I was a career student, always chasing the next goal. When I decided to go to school to become a dental assistant my dad stepped up, again. He paid my rent for a whole year so I could focus on school and being a mom. Sure, the rent was late every month, but it always came. Because he always came through. It's wild to think about how many beautiful, hilarious, and powerful memories we shared and it's even crazier to know that there were things coming storms we didn't see—that would try to overshadow it all. No matter what came next, I'll always remember the man who made me laugh, who made me strong, and who made me believe I could do anything, because I am my daddy's girl! Always.

Chapter Eight
FAMOUS NAME, SILENT PAIN

Being Thaddeus Matthews' daughter has never been for the weak. I didn't ask to be public. I didn't chase the spotlight. However, when your father is one of the most controversial voices in the city, you don't get much of a choice. The more bold and unfiltered he became, the more people he pissed off. My dad walked around Memphis like he was untouchable. Honestly, for a long time he kind of was untouchable.

He was proud of me, *so* proud. He bragged about me constantly, especially when he was just doing radio. I used to hop on his shows for fun, never expecting a dime, never asking for anything and people loved it. When I was on the mic with him, they saw a different side of Thaddeus Matthews; not the fire starter, not the hulk, but a father. A man who loved his daughter. They saw a human being. The show became so big, he got offered a television deal, and guess who they wanted, too? Me! A daddy-daughter duo, something Memphis had never seen before. As I write this, I'm tearing up, because maybe— *just maybe*—if I had said, "Yes," I could've saved him! Maybe I wouldn't be here now, trying to convince the world that he wasn't a monster. But I said, "No!" Not because of him. Never because of him. People already knew the name "Domonique Michelle Matthews"—he made sure of that, always saying my full name like it was royalty. Radio was different, and it didn't have a face. It gave me a little bit of privacy. A little bit of peace. TV, that was a whole different beast. I saw the comments. I saw the hate. Social media was *brutal* and I knew myself, I wasn't ready. I would have been ready to fight every single day. I wasn't mature enough to handle that kind of ignorance. Truth is, I still battle with it today. So, dad did the show on his own and he *killed* it. He made his money through advertising, and Lord, he was making a lot of it. Because love him or hate him, people watched and they listened. They couldn't look away. He was a force and I was his daughter. Trying to find my own way in a world that already had its eyes on me.

The *"Thaddeus Matthews Show"* on television. It was everything the radio show was and *more*. It had the same raw energy, the same fearless truth-telling, but now it had visuals and that changed everything. When my dad exposed someone, it wasn't just words anymore. He could show pictures. Receipts. Proof. When he promoted a business, it wasn't just a catchy slogan, it was a full-blown commercial. Professionally shot, edited, and aired to thousands of loyal viewers who trusted his word like gospel.

Trust me, his fans showed up. If my dad said a restaurant had the best wings in Memphis, that place would be packed the next day. If he said a mechanic was honest, people lined up. He wasn't just a media personality, he was a *movement*. Then there was the music. Instead of just playing the blues like he used to on the radio, he started hosting *Blues Shows*. Live events, real stages and real artists. He brought the soul of Memphis to life, blending entertainment with activism, business with culture, and always keeping his finger on the pulse of the people. Watching him build that empire, brick by brick, was something I'll never forget. He turned controversy into currency, and a microphone into a megaphone for truth. As for me, I was right there, watching, learning, and loving every minute of being Thaddeus Matthews' daughter.

When I used to do the radio show with him, it was all fun and games. Men would call in, flirting, asking to take me out, giving compliments and my dad would flip into full-on overprotective mode. Giving them the third degree on air like a sitcom dad. Asking about their salaries, how many kids they had, telling them they couldn't afford me. I'd roll my eyes and say, "Daddy, you make me sound like a gold digger!" But it was all in fun, or so I thought. When my dad advertised my businesses, he gave out my phone number and that's where things got real.

Let me tell you what happened. I was living in an apartment with just me and my son. Quiet, minding my business. I had just bought a new living room set, and a few delivery guys came to set it up. It was nothing unusual. They were in and out, they didn't say much, no weird vibes. They said they'd be back the next day to finish up a missing piece. A few hours later, my phone rang. It was a number I didn't recognize. I answered, and the voice on the other end said he was one of the delivery guys. He started describing himself, trying to jog my memory. I thought maybe he was calling about the furniture. Nope! He said, "I was calling to see if I could get to know you." Excuse me? You were just in my house. You had every chance to say something then. I asked him how he got my number, and he admitted—*he went through my paperwork at his job*. Creepy, right? I shut it down immediately. I told him I wasn't interested and hung up. I brushed it off, thinking, *"Loser."* The next day, the delivery guys came back. But he wasn't with them. Maybe he was too embarrassed to show his face. While the others were finishing up, I casually mentioned about the other delivery guy calling me. One of the guys who was bent over fixing the couch, stood up real fast, with his eyes wide opened. "What?" He told me that guy was new, transferred from another location for doing the same kind of thing, there. Then he said something that made my stomach drop. "You need to watch out for him. He's closer to you than you think." I was confused. I didn't know him nor I didn't see him around. Then the guy said, "Come here." He walked me to the window that looked out over the parking lot and pointed! "There, that's his car. He lives right there!" Directly across the street from me. I was speechless. No words. Just shock! That man had been watching me. He knew where I lived. He knew I was alone with my child and had the nerve to go through my personal information to call me.

Maybe I should have called the store and made a complaint right away. At the time, I had never experienced anything like it. I didn't know how to process it. Still, I started paying attention. Every time me and my son left the apartment, I'd notice him, that delivery guy leaving too. Always with a friendly "Hey!" I'd roll my eyes, gave a quick wave, and kept it moving. Then it became more than that. He would try to hold conversations while I was getting in my car. I'd give one word answers, I acted like I was always in a rush. I wasn't rude, but I wasn't welcoming either. Then one day, I was at the neighborhood grocery store with my son, and he approached me again. This time, apologizing for how he got my number and admitting it was wrong to go through my paperwork. He asked if he could take me out. I brushed him off again, told him I had a boyfriend (a lie), and walked away. Something about it didn't sit right. He was showing up *too much*, too often. There was a car wash about a block from my apartment on Riverdale. One summer day, I was there vacuuming my car. Music playing, my son wasn't with me. I was bent over cleaning the driver's side floor when I felt something like a shadow over me. I stood up, and there he was, *right there,* in my face. He was so close he could've kissed me. I shoved him hard and started cussing him out right there in the parking lot. People stopped. It was a whole scene. He was stalking me and he wanted me, that was it. I called the furniture store and told them everything. They assured me over and over that he was going to be let go. My dad stopped by the store himself to make his presence known. Loud and clear. Eventually, I moved into a new apartment. A new start and I never saw or heard from him again. But I'll never forget how that felt. How being *Thaddeus Matthews' daughter* made me visible in ways I didn't ask for and how I had to learn quickly, how to protect myself, even when the world thought I was already protected.

Every time something happened to me, my dad couldn't hold water. He'd always find a way to bring it up on his show making it *very* clear to his audience that I was *not* to be messed with. That was just who he was, loud, protective, and proud. Just like back in the radio days, I'd stop by the TV studio sometimes. I'd bring him food I cooked, just to hang out. We didn't talk every day life happens, we were both grown; but if I missed him, I knew exactly where to find him. Most days, you could catch him at Piccadilly's, posted up with his friends, the former mayor, or whatever "woman of the week" had his attention. When I stopped by the studio, I knew to have my makeup and hair on point. Because if I walked in, he was going to *let everybody know*. I could be sitting there, minding my business, waiting for a commercial break just to say hi and next thing I know, he's telling the producer, "Bring out a mic, Domonique Michelle, come on!" I'd act like I didn't come there for that, but it was our thing and people loved it. They got to put a face to the name he always said with so much pride. I always got good feedback from his fans—people who saw the softer side of him when I was around.

Then one day, I was watching his show from home. He opened the phone lines like he always did and this is Memphis, we're known for "checking." It's what we do. His fans would call in just to say something wild, hoping to get cussed out. It was part of the show. But this one caller took it too far. He said something so disrespectful, so out of line, it took my dad to a whole different level. You could see it in his face. He wasn't just mad—he was boiling. Like, ready to fight mad and the crazy part

78

is, people noticed. "Thats why I fuck your Daughter!" My mouth dropped, *"What?"* I was so pissed. Nobody I knew—*nobody*—would ever say something like that about me. This caller, this stranger; he crossed a line that should have never been touched. For my dad, it wasn't just a disrespectful call, it was a fight. Right there on live TV, he lost control and this wasn't entertainment anymore. These were fighting words. He was arguing over the phone, cussing like he was back on the block, coming out of his suit jacket, ready to throw hands through the screen. Memphis had found his weak spot, me! From that moment on, it became a trend. People realized that if you wanted to get under Thaddeus Matthews' skin, all you had to do was come for his daughter. Disrespect me, and you had him, every time. I still did the show with him now and then, but not as often and when I did, he wouldn't open the phone lines like he used to. I think he was scared—scared of what might be said, scared of what I might have to hear. Even when the lines were closed, I saw it on social media. The comments, the jokes, and the hate. Playing on my phone became a thing too, people calling, texting, trying to get a reaction. It started to wear on me. I was being recognized more and more, people who seemed to know my whole story, even when I hadn't told it. Then came the stalking, four more times. Four different situations, each one more disturbing than the last and by the time the last two happened, I was done. I was over it. Over the attention, over the fear, over the feeling that I couldn't just live my life without being watched, followed, or targeted. Being Thaddeus Matthews' daughter came with love, pride, and power; but it also came with a price and some days, that price felt way too high!

One night, I was dead asleep, I'm talking knocked out in that good sleep. You know the kind of sleep where your mouth is wide open, dreams sweet, body still. Then, ring ring, my phone went off. I answer it, half-sleep, eyes barely open. All I heard on the other end is moaning. Not just regular moaning, but nasty, creepy, intentional moaning. It was like somebody was getting off on calling me. I hung up quickly. My heart pounding now. The call came right back, the same moaning. Then, I heard it, my name, my name coming out of that pervert's mouth. I lost it. I cussed him out so bad, the devil probably blushed. I hung up again, but he kept calling; over and over, back to back. Every, damn night! After a while, I just got tired. I laid the phone face down on the dresser and let him moaned to himself until he got bored and eventually hung up. I was too exhausted to care. This madness went on for a month straight. Every night, like clockwork. That's when I realized, I couldn't escape it. I couldn't escape being a *Matthews*. Dating, please, that turned into a minefield. Most guys wouldn't date me, because they assumed dating me came with the drama of dealing with what I thought was, my father! As if you cheated on me, I would tell my dad and he would blast them on TV. Approaching me was a "no go" it seems; most would see me out and then inbox me on social media. This all could have been in my head, but that's what it felt like to me. Once they figured out who I was that he was my fathe, the whole vibe would shift. Some wondered if I was just as hard core as him. What started off as flirting and laughing over drinks would turn into, "So what's your daddy like in real life?" or "Yo, your dad really says that on air?" Instantly, I was turned off, mood killed. I started hating when some would introduce me as, "This is Thaddeus Matthews' daughter." Like that was my whole identity. Like I didn't have a name of my own. Like I wasn't somebody before or beyond being his daughter. I'm not just somebody's child, I am me. I've walked through hell with my heels on and came out with my own story. My own scars. My own damn voice. I love my daddy, don't get it twisted; but being his daughter came with a weight most people wouldn't understand. Sometimes, that weight looked like silence in the middle of the night, broken by a phone call I never asked for. I used to tell my friends what was happening. The late-night calls. The breathing. The moaning. The way he would say my name like he knew me like he wanted me.

They would listen, and they'd nod. Maybe offer a "girl, that's crazy," or "You need to change your number." But deep down, I could tell they didn't really understand me, not fully. I think they thought I was exaggerating, being dramatic. You know how people get when they can't wrap their heads around your kind of crazy. One night changed all of that, we were out late, just me, my girls, and my older sister. Music blasting, windows down, carefree vibes until my phone rang, it was an unknown number. Again, I already knew who it was. I said, "Y'all watch this." I put that call on speaker. The car went silent. Then came the moaning, slow, wet and nasty. Like a damn porn scene. Then my name. My government name, drawn out and heavy, like it meant something to him. I looked around the car, and the faces were shocked! Mouths open, and eyes wide. My best friend covered her mouth. Another girl looked like she was gonna throw up. Nobody said a word, they just listened. Then my sister snapped. She reached across me, snatched the phone, and let him have it. She called him every name you can think of and some you probably can't. She told him in graphic detail what she would do to him if she ever found out who he was. I mean, she painted a violent picture and you know what? That was the last time he ever called. Funny how that works. Sometimes it takes someone else losing their mind on your behalf to get the universe to listen. After that night, my friends saw it differently. They understood what I had been telling them. At least the surface of it, but what they didn't see is the part no one ever really sees that was the psychology of it. The way it was getting to my head. The way you start sleeping with the lights on, checking behind myself at night, and doubting every man who looks at you too long. The way it makes your skin crawl just hearing your own name whispered in the dark. Everybody was going through something, I get that and life is hard all around. The hardest part was going through something so *violating*, and still showing up like nothing is wrong. Still being the strong friend, the funny one and the one everybody leans on.

The trend of being my dad's target came from every direction—TV, social media, even just meeting new people. I always had to stay alert and I definitely wasn't the one you invited to your church, because chances were, my dad had already talked about your pastor on air.

Then came *her*. She was light-skinned, dark-haired, loud, and extra. The kind of woman who needed to be seen and my dad, he was the perfect man to give her a stage. She knew how to work her charm, and my dad, bless his heart, was blinded by her treats. Me being a woman, who knows how to work my charms; I knew from the moment we met, and she knew it too. She could never look me in the eye. She never tried to get close. I'm trying to say the heifer was there for money, the nicest way I can say it; because she wasn't there for love, she was there for opportunity! Lunches and dinners became their routine. She drove this beat-up two-door Saturn that looked like it belonged to a broke college freshman. Not long after, she had an apartment, in his name. When you're my dad's woman, his life becomes your life. So she was always at the TV studio, soaking it all in while he started grooming her.

Let me give you some backstory: it cost my dad $5,000 a month to keep his show on Comcast 31. That was his grind. It wasn't long before she had her own show fully funded, of course, by my dad. I don't know how or when their relationship ended. I'd like to believe he finally saw through her. For me it ended, as soon as it started because my daddy was married and she was just a sidepiece. Although I didn't care for the woman, I never believed any woman deserved that kind of exposure. So when I saw what my dad posted, I had to call him. As usual one evening, my DM's started going off and phone began to rang with the "Girl, yo daddy is so crazy!" I knew again my dad had done something to send social media crazy, but this time he even shocked me with this one. Now as a woman I completely go against what my dad did. When I open Facebook my jaw drops, and my eyes buck. There it was, a complete nude picture of this lady posted by my father. Going viral, constantly being re-share, being commented on, and joked about. Of course, I called him, no "hello." Just, "Daddy, what the hell?" Like he hadn't done anything wrong, he calmly said, **"She said she was gonna post pictures of *me*, so I wasn't gonna wait. I posted mines first."** My *crazy* daddy. I couldn't do anything but laugh half in disbelief, half because that was just him. Of course, he wasn't even at home. He was at an ex-girlfriend's house, and now they were arch enemies, too. She was about to learn what a lot of people already knew: my dad didn't have much to lose, and that's exactly why people didn't mess with him. The very next day, the fallout began. She was fired from her job turns out she was a teacher's assistant at a local community college. Then came the eviction. Her things were out on the street, and yes, he took pictures, and yes they were posted. From there, it spiraled. For years, they went back and forth, false charges, lawsuits, and public drama. Any platform that would give her a mic, she was on it. Somehow, she even got voted in as a school board district leader. Even in that "upstanding" position, she turned it into a circus. A full-blown embarrassment and honestly, the city of Memphis has my father to thank for that mess. He gave her the spotlight. He gave her the stage. Now, I know what you're thinking: "But what does this have to do with *you*?" One night sleep in the middle of the night, my phone was constantly going off "unknown caller." I have dealt with this still long enough to not entertain private calls. But after so many calls I answer with all the attitude. "What!" On the other end a woman, with a sassy tone, "Oh, did I wake you? Did I wake you from sucking your daddy's dick?" You can't make this up! A grown ass woman playing on her ex-boyfriend daughter's phone. In so much shock, I calmly said, "You know I'll beat your ass!" Once again… another situation that had *nothing* to do with me, and yet, here I was the target. All because of my father's choices. Now let me tell you something, baby! The devil don't waste his time on folks who ain't got purpose. No ma'am. He comes for God's best soldiers, and if you feel like he is coming at you hard, you best believe there's an anointing over your life. I know, because I've lived it.

There was a time when the weight of it all nearly crushed me. I was working customer service at a bank, 10am to 7pm shift. My routine, most mornings, I'd drop my baby boy off at school and head straight to work. This day, this day was different. Before I get to that, let me catch you up. I had already been through five, yes five different stalking situations. I had just moved into a new apartment complex, thinking maybe I'd finally find peace. However, peace didn't come easy. I already was receiving the pervert who was calling, masturbating to my name on the phone. Then I started getting love letters on my windshield, balloons tied to my mirror. Somebody was watching. Watching me, too closely. They knew it was just me and my son. No company. No noise. Just us. This day, I was actually in a good mood. I was running a little behind, so I dropped my son off and came back home to finish getting dressed. I walked in, singing a song I'd just heard on the radio, walking down my hallway to my bedroom, feeling light. Then I turned the corner into my bedroom and froze. There he was, a man dressed in all black. No mask, and no gloves. Just standing there beside my bed like he belonged. Light brown skin, maybe 5'6", low haircut. We both scared each other. You could tell, he wasn't expecting me back. I was scared, but I stood tall and in a demanding tone "What the hell are you doing in my house?" He raised his hands, calm as still water. "Don't move," Me, I was still stuck. He repeated again, "Don't move." He took one step toward me and baby, before that foot hit the ground, I was gone. I turned and ran like my life depended on it, because it did. He chased me, but I didn't stop. I ran straight to the leasing office. Two men saw him chasing behind me and took off after him into another direction. I burst into the office, breathless, shaking. "I caught a man in my bedroom," I cried. They called the police. I called my big sister who alerted the family. Then I called my Daddy. Baby, before I could blink, the whole street was lit up with police cars. My family and my Daddy who was raising holy hell. Baby, let me tell you, when you've been through enough, there comes a moment when you just snap. Not out of fear, but out of resolve. That day, I reached mines. Right in front of my apartment was a tennis court, two kids and what I assumed was their daddy used to be out there every day, practicing like they were training for Olympics, all day, every day. While the police were dusting for fingerprints and walking through

86

my place, that man, the father stopped one of the officers. He said, "I don't want to get involved," but then pointed straight to the door the man had ran into, and you guessed it. That man lived in the same complex. His apartment was positioned right across the street from mines. He could looked out his window, and he could see mines. Every move, every light switch, every time I came or went. I was being watched like a hawk, and I didn't even know it. I had no words, and no tears. Just a deep, bone-tired *fed up*. The police couldn't enter his apartment without proper cause. So the security guards came up with a plan. They told him the office got an anonymous call about smoke coming from his unit. Just a way to get him to open the door and get his information while the police were still on-site. It worked. He had no warrants, and because they didn't actually catch him inside my house. They couldn't arrest him. As for me, I was done. I sat there thinking about my son and about how close I came to not being able to protect him. I thanked God, *truly* thanked Him that my baby wasn't home that day. I argue with my Daddy and my Mama. They were begging me to stay somewhere else until the man was caught. I was dead set on, "No, I'm not running. I'm not hiding." I decided it was time to go buy a gun. Because, I'm a mother and my job is to protect my child. My son was not going to be scared in his own home. Period!

I was on my way to the gun store, phone pressed to my ear, talking to my dad as he stayed behind until the police finished with my house, until he suddenly went quiet. Then he said, low and sharp, *"I think I'm looking at the muthafucka."* My heart dropped. He meant *him*—the man I caught inside my house. Now, here he was, strolling past my father like it was nothing. He saw the police, he saw my family but apparently he realize it was nothing they could do. I was mad as hell. But my dad, he was livid. All he needed was a name. Now he had a face. That night, my dad went on his show and told the whole city of Memphis what happened. He didn't hold back, he put the man's face and full criminal record on blast and he wasn't at least a bit cautious to let everyone know that he had done this to me. Turns out, the guy had a rap sheet longer than Winchester Avenue. I watched the show, and I didn't know whether my dad was being brave or reckless. I couldn't understand was this for entertainment or being an overprotective dad. I know I didn't like it, because while he was telling the truth, he was also putting me in the spotlight. My safety became tonight's headline and the man still hadn't been arrested, yet. That night I didn't sleep. How could I? My dad literally put a target on my back. I found out the apartment he was staying in wasn't even his. He was living with a woman and her three small kids. Because of what he did, she had 72 hours to move out. I became paranoid. I felt violated by the man who broke into my home, and by my father, who made it public. I didn't go anywhere without my gun on my hip or within reach. I was constantly on edge. The stories I've told you, they barely scratch the surface. Being Thaddeus Matthews' daughter isn't something I chose; but I'm surviving it? That's something I do every day.

There was the girl my dad cursed out on air, she didn't

88

come for him, she came for me. Made a whole Facebook group asking people to vote on whether I was male or female. Like my identity was a joke. Like I wasn't human. Then there was the so-called activist, who went live claiming he'd been with me, Thaddeus Matthews' daughter. He lied for clout, then came back and apologized like that could undo the damage. Like his words didn't stick to me like scars. I tried to escape it. I packed up and tried to move to California, hoping to start fresh somewhere no one knew my name. But my dad, broke down crying. He told me I was all he had and just like that, I stayed. Not because I wanted to, but because I didn't want to break him. Every day, I walked out the door like I was unbothered. Like I was strong, but inside I wanted to run. I wanted to disappear. I wanted to be *me* not someone's daughter, not someone's target, not someone's storyline. I'm still here, still standing, and still surviving.

Chapter Nine
HE BROKE ME

For years, I watched my father, Thaddeus Matthews turn a blind eye to the quiet warnings his body whispered. He wore strength like a second skin, brushing off symptoms with a shrug and a deep laugh. But I saw it. The way his steps grew slower. The way his eyes sometimes looked far away, like he was trying to outrun something he couldn't quite name. Diabetes started as a condition we thought we could manage. Something you control with willpower and routine. But slowly, it morphed into something darker, something we had to witness with helpless hands due his own pride. It became the third presence in the room, silent, steady, and unforgiving. My father, the man who built his brand with bare hands and bold dreams as an entrepreneur; but in a system where healthcare is a luxury, his lack of insurance meant every doctor visit was a financial tug-of-war. So, he chose what he always did; he chose work, he chose his show. He put his health in the corner, like an overdue bill you don't want to look at. This man, who once called me his "whole world," who told anyone who'd listen that I had him wrapped around my finger just by way I say "Daddy," was slowly becoming someone else. Still present, still raw and unfiltered, but dimmed. As if the spotlight that had once shined so bright on our lives was flickering, unsure of its power. I clung to every story he told. Every look and every quiet moment between us. I stayed his little girl, even when he was too tired to notice. Because even as the man I knew faded, the love he once gave me he started to forget. For years, I watched him become a legend, exposing truths, dragging skeletons out of closets on live air. All that spotlight came with shadows, the more truth he told, the less he trusted. I guess when you expose that much, you start to wonder who might expose you. He was the oldest of five, but you wouldn't know it by the way his life started. My grandmother gave him up to her older sister, and because she didn't raised him, their relationship felt more like siblings than mother and son. I remember watching her in hospice, fragile but still fiery. I'd sneak away on my lunch breaks just to sit with her, listen to her stories, her gospel hums and her cussing. Lord, she was a great cusser. It's probably where I got my love for salty-tongued elders. It was on her deathbed that something shifted. My father said that was the first time ever she told him she loved him and said she was proud of him. Not long after that, she slipped away. I always felt after finally getting that love from her, he grew angry. He didn't cry not then, not in front of me; but I saw it in the way he stared past the walls. Like a little boy who just found out the world isn't as kind as he'd hoped. We thought she had a life insurance policy. What we didn't know was that borrowing against it meant there was nothing left to pay out. He turned to his siblings, hoping for help, and maybe for the first time, he felt like they were holding back. I don't know all the details, but after her funeral, they all went estrange, and he went so far to try to show everyone that he paid for the funeral by putting on her tombstone from your son Thaddeus Matthews.

Birthdays used to be our thing. I'd gather people, plan little celebrations. Eventually, they stopped feeling like celebrations. It was just me, him, and a few folks from the club. So he changed them, turned them into blues shows, louder and flashier. He transformed into something else entirely. "Thaddy Bear" faded, and "The Cussing Pastor" took the stage. A man with a preacher's cadence and a firebrand's fury. The name stuck. The controversy stuck harder. He remarried for the ninth time. That woman started soft, sugar-voiced and bright-eyed; but like most people in my father's world, she evolved or maybe unraveled. She became harder, and sharper.

As my father's brand shifted, the fire that once made him a household name, started to dim. The money didn't come the way it used to. The interviews were fewer, the headlines louder, but short-lived. Even though, his spotlight began to fade, mine started to flicker into view. I watched what he went through with my grandmother. The emotional debt that came from not having certain protections in place, that pain lit a fire in me. I carved out my own path as a life insurance broker, opened a beautiful office in the heart of downtown, and for once, I felt like I had found my thing. I was thriving and I was making something out of nothing. Just like he had done. Life doesn't call ahead. Just as a four-year relationship was crumbling at my feet, I found out I was pregnant with my second child. I panicked. I was already raising a teenager, my oldest son a high schooler with dreams of his own. Now here I was, in my 30s, staring at five pregnancy tests, each one a silent scream. People always said I was strong, and I was; but this demanded something else. This required a level of strength I hadn't even known how to ask for. Then the pandemic hit. The world folded in on itself. Businesses closed. My relationship dissolved completely. I was pregnant and painfully alone. Depression crept in like an unwelcome visitor that refused to leave. I cried in closets, trying to protect my son from the weight of my unraveling. Some days, I questioned whether I could keep doing any of it. Whether I wanted to. But God, and my boys, those two hearts I brought into this world, they saved me. They reminded me that no one would ever care for them the way I would. I chose them. I chose life. I found a therapist, and for my entire pregnancy, counseling became my sanctuary. A standing appointment with the version of me that refused to quit.

When the world reopened, so did my hustle. I went full throttle, I used every ounce of my financial savvy helping small businesses receive pandemic grants, and just right before my delivery making a cool 25k giving myself the ability to enjoy new motherhood again and I stayed home with my new son until he was 8 months old. I was in straight mommy mode. But after nearly two years of not being able to work my business, I gave it a try again, but it was too hard to do with a new baby alone, my passion for insurance dried up like, a well I had drawn from too many times. I started searching again.

Now, I'm a single mother of two and eventually I had to expand to a bigger place. Rent was as high as $2,100 a month. My oldest was entering his senior year. I found myself working three jobs, seven days a week, barely catching my breath, and my lupus felt like it was going to kill me everyday. To everyone else it seems, I never missed a beat. My smile has stretch marks. My ambition has bags under its eyes.

My daddy never knew I was working three jobs. He never knew the weight I carried, or how often I stood on stages of responsibility where applause never came. He would've called me strong, and he'd be right. Not even he could've imagined just how deep my strength ran. I work for IRS from home, from 8am to 4pm. Then I picked up my son from daycare and work at Amazon from 6pm to 6:30am, Monday thru Friday. Then I was a waitress on Saturdays and Sundays at a local breakfast spot, being tired was an understatement.

As the years stretched forward, my father's body became more fragile; but you wouldn't know it from the way he walked into an ER. Every visit felt like a show. The nurses, the doctors, they all gave him the celebrity treatment. He'd crack jokes, flirt with the staff, talk like a man who was just stopping by, not one battling diabetes as it slowly turned into heart failure. Beneath that charm was fear, real quiet fear. The kind that doesn't speak unless spoken to. Every time they tried to admit him, he would argue. Loud and dramatic, he was my father to the core. He'd push back against the doctors, the nurses, even his wife, refusing to be seen as weak, as sick. But I had my way, I'd slide into the conversation with that running joke we shared, "Daddy, don't you dare leave me

I'm too cute to be an orphan." That line made him pause and roll his eyes. I pretend I was annoyed, and it worked. Even if just for one night, he would stay, for me. His wife was a blessing in those days. A real partner in the fight. She carried a binder of meds like it was gospel. She knew every dosage, every side effect, and always kept me informed, even when I couldn't be there. Truthfully, I couldn't always be there. I had a full plate. A toddler, a teenager, bills stacked like playing cards, and a calendar that never stopped. I loved my father fiercely, but I was stretched thin pulled in every direction. Unfortunately, guilt became a companion. Love battled with exhaustion. She held it down when I couldn't, and I was grateful. Even though my hands were full, my heart never stopped making space for him, between two boys, three jobs, and rent that felt like robbery, I was running on fumes. That apartment the one with sky-high costs and low joy had to go. I knew I deserved better, and more importantly, my boys deserved more than an overworked mother. So, on my birthday, I signed the lease to our new home, four bedrooms. It was more than just a house, it was a reward. A symbol that all those sleepless nights, closet cries, and nonstop hustling hadn't been in vain. I stood in that empty living room with my boys and breathed, "Thank You God," not knowing I was about to be forever changed afterwards.

When Daddy's wife called to tell me she was rushing him to the E.R. for chest pains, my heart sank, but I couldn't move. Normally, I'd drop everything, no questions asked, but that week was different. My son's father was trippin again, and my son had to stay home from child care, I was working my remote job with my little one beside me. The world had reopened, but hospitals were still strict, no children allowed, no exceptions. Still, I stayed connected. Constant calls and updates, heart pacing faster with each one. The doctors wanted to admit him, said he needed more care. But Daddy was dead set on staying out; he had a blues show the next day and was worried if word got out that he was in the hospital, ticket sales would tank. He couldn't afford that hit, not now. Turns out, it was a mild heart attack. He was released that night and like always, we were back on the phone, texting, and checking in. His humor never faded, his voice still full of life. So he took the worry from me and to me my dad was super tough. It was my birthday weekend and it was also the blues show was a celebration for my dad's wife birthday.

That Saturday, someone had already asked me out on a date. I hadn't done anything for myself in a while, so I got dressed, tried on joy like a borrowed outfit. Right as I was finishing my hair, daddy called. "Hey, your sister and the boys just stopped by, come over." "Aww man daddy, I'm sorry. I'm about to go on a date." "A date?" He said, his voice dipping into playful jealousy. "Yeah, tell everyone I love them, I'll catch y'all next time." There was a pause, and to my daddy that meant cancel your date. "Little girl, I need to put my eyes on you." "I'm coming, daddy, I'll stop by soon." From time to time that night my dad called to check on me, because that night a crazy guy was driving around Memphis shooting random people for no reason, and was taking police on a high speed chase for the rest of the night.

Sunday morning came like clockwork. I worked the breakfast shift, got off early enough to enjoy the rest of the day, feeling that buzz of something new on the horizon. On my ride home, I passed a furniture spot and stopped on a whim. They sold appliances and Lord knows, I needed everything: stove, fridge, washer, and dryer. But fate has timing, and I caught a deal on a washer and dryer, I couldn't ignore. It ate up all my money, but I felt proud. I was building my home. Still, practicality kicked in, I needed just a little buffer: gas money, groceries, and the small things life always demands. So I did what I'd always done, I called daddy. "Hey, Daddy, I just bought a washer and dryer for the house, but it took all my money. Can I have $100 in case the boys need something?" Instead of the usual, "You know I got you, baby girl," I got silent. Then he said, "How you going to ask me for money when I just got out the hospital?" I laughed, confused. "Daddy, what does you getting out the hospital have to do with me asking for $100?" He snapped. "Nawh, I ain't got no money for you, I got bills." I froze. It wasn't like him. He'd always joked, always teased, but never shut me down like that. Maybe, I sounded bratty. Maybe I caught him on the wrong day. But in that moment, I wasn't his little girl I was just another bill he couldn't afford. We hung up quickly. No warmth. No comfort. I rode home gripping the steering wheel like a lifeline. My head was spinning and my heart was bruised. Somewhere between that phone call and the next red light, I made a decision; fine, I'll find a fourth job. This is why I don't ask for help, because even heroes have limits, even daddy, my Daddy!

Monday morning, I was halfway clocked in at my remote job, coffee lukewarm, attention scattered. Just another day of juggling work and life. As usual, I scrolled through Facebook for a quick break and there it was a post from Daddy. He had taken a picture of my older sister, blown it up real big like she was being honored, and then wrote a caption that felt more like a dig than a celebration. Something about how she had come to see him in the hospital, how she'd been bonding with his wife and then the line that slapped sideways: *"Meanwhile, I got a daughter asking me for money that I ain't even laid eyes on."* I blinked. Honestly, I wasn't even mad, not really. It didn't stab me in the heart, it just felt petty. It felt like high school hallway petty. I wasn't expecting public shade from my own father, but there it was: his post, his platform, his way of talking slick. I commented, plain and simple: "Wow." Then I shot him a text. Our messages had started to shift lately. They didn't feel like father-daughter anymore. They felt like the kind you get from an ex; jealous, dramatic, laced with that "I miss you, but I won't say it" energy. The irony is, I hadn't ghosted him. I was just living, working, parenting, and surviving. Somehow, my absence became ammunition. That text thread read less like love and more like tension in disguise. I remember sitting there staring at my phone, wondering how we got here. Daddy, the man who once bragged that I had him wrapped around my finger, now throwing shade because I didn't show up fast enough, and because I asked for help. I guess sometimes, even when you're a daddy's girl, you learn that love doesn't always come easy. Especially when pride and pain share the same room. My father was the kind of man who could command a room with just one sentence. Proud, charismatic, and loud in every way, especially when it came to not admitting vulnerability. So when he didn't have something, he wouldn't just say it. Instead, he would twist it, flip it, and turn it around until somehow you felt bad for even asking. That day, after texting back and forth and going nowhere, I picked up the phone. He was convinced I didn't want to see him. That I was intentionally keeping my distance, but that was the farthest thing from the truth. I loved him and I always did. He had his world, and I had mines: bills, babies, shifts, and struggles. There was love, but there wasn't always bandwidth and honestly, I was tired. Tired of everything becoming his show headline. Tired of my private life making public cameos. So I started keeping more to myself. So when I called, it was fireworks. He wanted to talk, and so did I, but neither of us wanted to listen first. It was a verbal ping-pong match. Two strong personalities, each one trying to out-speak the other. He was stubborn as ever. As for me, I was holding my ground for once. On that phone call, my father met his match. We over-talked and under-heard. However, beneath the static, there was something tender a shared frustration, a lingering love, and two people who only knew how to scream what they should've whispered. We were alike, that was the problem and maybe that was also the answer. The argument had been going on for a while loud, heated, and familiar. Yet, in the middle of the shouting, I heard something that shattered me in a way I didn't expect. He called me a **"bitch."** My father, the man I once adored. The man I used to call my hero called me a bitch. I went silent. Completely shut down. My hands were still on the steering wheel, but my heart was somewhere else cracked wide open. I pulled into a gas station, parked the car, and just broke. My forehead rested against the wheel as the tears came hard and fast. I couldn't hold them back anymore. In that moment, I texted him, "Now I understand why I loved [baby daddy's name], because he was you. The argument felt so familiar the name-calling, the belittling, the mani-pulation." For years, I had been fighting a silent war in a relationship that was mentally abusive and growing physically dangerous and I kept it all inside. I wore strength like armor, because showing weakness felt like giving up. No one seemed to care, but me. So I stayed quiet.

The next day, my best friend called to check on me. She always knows when something's off. That night, I tried to take a break from social media, to breathe, and to heal even just a little. Unfortunately, my father didn't. He took the text I sent him, my raw, vulnerable truth and posted it on Facebook. A screenshot with the caption: **"When your kids feel entitled."** That was the moment I realized, I wasn't just hurt, I was betrayed. Hot-headed just like my father, I picked up the phone and called his wife. We had grown close over the years, so I didn't hold back. "Can you tell your damn husband to keep my name out of his mouth?" She had me on speakerphone and just like that, it was on. Two Matthews, going at it in true Matthews fashion loud, sharp, and unfiltered. Then he

100

said it: "I'm gonna put on a show with you." I fired back without hesitation, "Go ahead. But when you do, make sure you say this too, you're dead to me. You have no children." See, I wasn't scared of him. Not even a little. I knew that man inside and out. I knew his patterns, his pride, and his pain. What he didn't know and what no one knew was that I was already fighting demons in silence. I was exhausted, not just tired, but soul-deep weary. He was hurt, because for the first time I didn't drop everything to rush to the hospital. He had no idea what it was costing me just to keep breathing, to keep showing up, and to keep pretending I was okay. It's impossible to keep showing up for everyone else when you're the only one showing up for *you*. After everything, after the shouting, the name-calling, the betrayal, I broke. I had to call my village. My best friends, my cousins, my sisters, and my momma. The cry that came out of me wasn't just about that moment, it was a lifetime of holding it all in. I had lost my father, not to death, but to something just as final: disappointment. The tears wouldn't stop. Then came the posts, one after another.

"When your kids feel entitled. When you've done all you can for your child. The show is at 7 p.m." He was building it up like a performance. A show for the world to watch. The man who once loved his daughter was now using every word he could to destroy her, publicly. As 7 p.m. approached, I felt the weight of it all pressing down on me. My inbox and DMs were blowing up. People were watching, people were judging, and people were choosing sides in a war, I never wanted. Then, without asking without knocking, they came; my momma, my

101

sisters, my besties, and my village. They walked through the door with liquor, love, and fire in their eyes. "You not watching that bullshit." They were right. God knew what I needed. This wasn't a battle I could fight alone. Not this time. Sometimes, even the strongest daughters need someone to hold them up when their world falls apart. I told myself I wouldn't watch it. I had my village around me, holding me up, pouring drinks, drowning out the noise. But five minutes before the so-called "show" was set to end, curiosity or maybe hope got the best of me. I clicked in and there he was, my father on live with tears streaming down his face. For a moment, my heart softened maybe he was about to take it back. Maybe he realized the damage he had done. Maybe he missed me. Then I heard him say it, "Domonique was jealous of her sister. She always wanted to be the only child." Just like that, the knife twisted deeper. He didn't just hurt me, he rewrote my story. He painted me as bitter, selfish, and envious and he did it with tears in his eyes, like *he* was the one who had been betrayed. He didn't know the battles I was fighting. The silence I was drowning in. The strength it took just to keep breathing. He didn't know that I had spent my whole life trying to be enough for him, and for everyone. Now, in front of the world, he reduced me to a jealous child. The noise that followed his "show" was deafening. Who does that? Who creates a public spectacle to tear down their own flesh and blood? Their own child? My inbox was flooded. My DMs wouldn't stop. The comments, God, the comments. Strangers were judging me like they knew my life. Like they knew my heart. "How dare she not go to the hospital?" "After all he's done for her?" One time, I missed *one* time. After showing up fifty times before. After being the one who always dropped everything. After being the one who never complained, but no one saw that. No one saw me working three jobs I was overqualified for, seven days a week, just to keep us afloat after the pandemic crushed my business. No one saw me pushing through lupus flares, pretending I wasn't in pain. No one saw me raising a brilliant son, an athlete with a 4.0 GPA and a full ride to college or my baby boy, thriving, happy, and loved. I was doing everything for everyone with barely any support from the two men I loved, most. Now, I was being dragged, publicly on Facebook, on Instagram and on YouTube, where his show had over 100,000 subscribers. I wanted to scream! Strangers were walking up to me in public, telling me they were praying for me. Sharing stories about their fathers, some meant well and some just wanted the tea. Everywhere I went, I was *recognized*; not for my strength, and not for my resilience. I was recognized for the pain someone else broadcasted. You can't make this shit up! Out of all the messages flooding my inbox, one hit different, one made my blood boil. It was from a woman I'd seen around before never close, just familiar. She messaged me, "Do you need me to let you borrow $100 until you get paid?" Breathe, Domonique, breathe girl. I've been a lot of things in my life, but backing down from a fight that has never been one of them. Still, I had to remind myself who I was. I had to remember my son, my family, and my name. When it came to social media, I always moved with them in mind. I never wanted to do anything that would make them ashamed of me. Because truth be told, there were times I was ashamed of *him*, my father. When he would come for people online, dragging them for views, for laughs, for clout; I felt for those people. I wanted to stop him; but I couldn't. Now, I was one of them. He had gotten to a place where no one was off limits, not strangers, not friends, and not even his own daughter. All for ratings. All for a show and the world was watching.

A whole year had passed, and I hadn't spoken to my father. Every now and then, I would peek at his page just to see if he was still breathing, still talking, and still being *him*. I didn't reach out, I couldn't. I had lost my biggest headache and somehow, my biggest heartbreak too. Everything that reminded me of him, I wanted no parts of it. The Steelers, that used to be *our* team. Now, I couldn't even look at their colors without feeling sick. Entrepreneurship, that dream died with the last piece of hope I had in him. I didn't want to build anything anymore. I was too hurt, and too angry and the questions haunted me. **Why does every man I love do me like this? Why can't I trust a man?** I wasn't just mourning my father, I was mourning the little girl who believed in him. The woman who kept trying to find pieces of him in other men, only to be broken again and again.

September was the month my father did the show. Now, it's the month my world cracked open, the month my dad shattered everything I thought was solid between us. From that moment on, I carried the silence like a second skin. I made it through the rest of the year, through the falling summer, without a single word from him. Still, every time I peek in on him, whether in memory or on his page, the hurt and the anger hit just as hard as they did that first day. No one ever talks about grieving a person who is still alive. Holiday's came and went and I thought about him, but I just couldn't. My dad had four kids, two girls, and two boys. One of them, I was never quite sure about. He didn't look like us, didn't feel like us. My sister and I tried to reach out to him at our grandmother's burial, but he made it clear: he wanted nothing to do with us. I never saw him again until he was lying in a casket, taken by a drunk driver. But the rest of us, you could look at us and see it; we were blood. All three of us blind, all three of us carrying about 50% of that unmistakable Matthews attitude. Let's just say, you didn't want to be on our bad side. I was the baby. My dad never hid who his favorite was and I carried that guilt like a shadow. My sister and I would try time and time again, to bring us all together for dinner. Unfortunately, every time it ended the same. My brother and my dad are two sides of the same coin, both with egos too big to fit in the same room. One of them always stormed out. My sister was the quiet one, until daddy would say something to piss her off. As for me, I was a little bit of everyone, the spark and the storm. I had hoped that one day that we would all just be family not estrange people who all shared the same DNA. Even in the silence between my father and I, I was still the name they used when they wanted to get under his skin. That summer, I was sent a video, just a live clip. A man I had never heard of, calling himself an activist in Memphis, was live with a group of other men, smoking and having I guess a guy session. I didn't know him. I never met him and I hadn't heard of him. However, apparently, he and my dad were enemies. The whole conversation was about checking my dad, that's what they called it. Somehow, it didn't stay about him. Somehow, I became the topic, Thaddeus Matthews' daughter, me.

Once again, I was dragged into something that had nothing to do with me. Once again, I was the easiest way to hurt him, because they all knew no matter how broken things were between us, no matter how long the silence stretched, I was still the one who could make him feel something and that's what hurt the most. Even when I wasn't speaking to him, even when I was trying to heal, I was still being used as a pawn in his wars. I was still being disrespected, not for who I am, but for who I belong to and I didn't ask for that. I was just his daughter, the one who used to be his baby. The one who still carries the weight of being loved too loudly, then left too quietly. There he is, "I fuck the shit out Thaddeus Matthews' daughter, that bitch stay in my inboxes." Another guy, "You know she don't fuck with him no more!" They proceeded to make jokes on how his own daughter want nothing to do with him. It was just stupid. Still burning with anger toward my dad, I decided this time I wasn't going to stay silent. When they did this crap on the show, over the phone, I didn't have a name or a face but this was different. Yeah, he was still my father and I was done letting people use me as a punching bag just to get at him. So when that so-called activist in Memphis decided to run his mouth about me on a livestream, me being a person he didn't even know, I made sure to respond. I pulled up my receipts. I screenshot my inbox to show the world we had never spoken, never exchanged a word. I posted it right on my timeline for everyone to see. No confusion. No mystery. Then I went in, I tagged him directly. I made sure he saw it. I made sure he knew I wasn't hiding behind anything. If you're bold enough to speak on me, be bold enough to stand in it and just like that, he folded. Suddenly, he was confused acting like he didn't know I existed. "I didn't know he had a daughter this fine," he said. "My bad." "Your bad? Nigga please, keep your beef man to man." It was weak as hell to bring me into it. That's the problem. People think they can throw dirt on your name, disrespect you in public, and then walk it back like it's nothing. I'm not the one to play with, not anymore. I may still be hurting. I may still be angry at my dad, but I will never let anyone use me as a weapon again.

November came, and it had been over a year since I'd spoken to my dad, not a word since last September. The silence between us had grown thick, and heavy like a wall I didn't know how to climb anymore. My brother came into town and wanted to see everyone. I agreed to stop by, but I made it clear I wasn't coming if dad was going to be there. They promised me he would come at a different time. They said they make sure we didn't cross paths. So there I was, in the living room, laughing, and really laughing with my sister and brother. For a moment, it felt like old times. I even said, "Let's take a picture before y'all's daddy gets here," half-joking, half-bracing myself and just as the camera clicked, there was a knock at the door, in walked my father. It was the first time I'd seen him in over a year. My whole body tensed. The laughter died in my throat. I felt the irritation rise like fire under my skin, that was my cue. I stood up, hugged and kissed everyone in the room, said my goodbyes with a smile that didn't reach my eyes and walked right past the man who gave me life like he was a stranger on the street, not a glance and not a word. In the car, the tears came fast. My hands shook on the steering wheel, because no matter how strong I tried to be, no matter how cold I acted in that moment, he didn't understand. He didn't understand that a part of me died, the day he betrayed me and I'm still mourning her. What I didn't know was that my silence, my coldness cut him just as deep. My dad used Facebook like a diary sometimes and one day, there it was, a post, a confession. He wrote that he didn't realize the damage he was doing when he aired that show that he knew, before he left this world, he had to make things right with me. He started asking his fans, and his followers to reach out to me to try and get me to talk to him to fix what was broken. He started to start his show with a picture of me, and in every show he continued to ask people to reach out to me. We were both hurting. We were both reaching in our own ways, but I didn't believe we were fixable. One day at work my phone rang, and right there for the first time my daddy called. My soul dropped and I had to excuse myself to not show the tears that were building up in my eyes. I didn't answer. What the hell would I say? How could I trust him again? The respect I had for him was gone and when that left, it felt like my father left with it. The man I

108

knew, the man I loved, he would have never thrown me out like that. He would have never made me feel like I was disposable. Still, to this day, I've never watched that show, because I know if I do, I will break all over again.

Dear Me,

I know you're hurting right now. I know you're sitting in a silence that feels louder than any argument ever could. I know you miss him, your dad and I know how much it hurts to admit that out loud. You didn't deserve what happened. The betrayal, the public pain, the feeling of being thrown away by the one man who was supposed to protect you no matter what. That wound cut deep, and it's okay that you haven't healed yet. It's okay that you're angry. It's okay that you're confused. It's okay that you miss him and still don't know if you can ever trust him again. You're not weak for feeling both love and pain at the same time. You're not broken because you want to reach out and also want to protect your heart. You're human. You're a daughter, and you're grieving the version of your father you thought would never hurt you.

But I want you to know this: you are not defined by his mistakes. You are not responsible for fixing what he broke. You are allowed to take your time. You are allowed to feel everything, and you are allowed to choose peace, even if that means keeping your distance. One day, you'll look back and see how strong you were for standing in your truth. For not pretending it didn't hurt. For loving him from afar, even when it felt impossible. You're still his daughter. More importantly, you are your own woman and you are worthy of love, respect, and healing. Hold on. You're going to be okay!

With love,
Your Future Self

Chapter Ten
SEX, SICKNESS & SADNESS

I missed his call and I miss him. The man I could make laugh with just my charm. The man who, every time he looked at me, saw himself. I told myself, "If he calls again, I'll answer." One night, I was sitting with my youngest son's father. My phone lit up. **"Daddy"** My favorite picture of us filled the screen. I answered, "Hello?" On the other end, **"Domonique Michelle Matthews,"** a deep breath. "Yes?" "This is your father." "I know, daddy." Just like that, the little girl in me the one who waited, who wondered, who ached began to speak. He spoke first, "I have you on the air." He said it like it was nothing, but to me, it was everything. **"I feel the disrespect I gave you should be matched by the size of my apology."** Right there, on YouTube, on Facebook, in front of his audience, he began to apologize. He tried to explained and I just listened. Tears streamed down my face; but as a Matthews, I showed no weakness in my voice. It was time. Time to tell my father the damage he did, calmly and slowly. I said, **"You broke me. You hurt me. I always had your back right or wrong. You threw me away. You killed me inside."** I had a way of making my daddy listen, because before I could forgive him, he needed to understand. "The one man who was put on this earth to protect me threw me away. If I can't believe in you, daddy, what man can I ever believe in?" As I sat there, talking to my daddy on the air, I watched the views climb. One by one, hundreds, then thousands and when our conversation ended, so did his show. Just like that, but something didn't sit right in me. Was it real? Or was my most vulnerable moment just another episode for ratings? Another show for the world to watch, react to, and move on from while I was left holding the weight of it all; I looked over at my son's father, a man who had lost his own dad. I thought surely he would understand. I thought he would hold space for me, but what I got was coldness, silence and judgment. That **Matthews** in me, yeah, she came out and his ass had to go. I needed peace. Not pity. Not performance. So I spent the rest of the night on my porch. Just me, a bottle of wine, and gospel music playing low in the background. Don't judge me, I needed that moment to think, to feel and to breathe, because healing doesn't always look like tears and hugs. Sometimes, it looks like a woman sitting alone under the stars, trying to make peace with her father's voice and a lifetime of silence. After that conversation on the air, months passed, and silence returned. It was familiar and heavy. Then one day, I was driving down Germantown Parkway. My phone rang and it was *her,* my Dad's wife. Confusion hit me like a wave, because she never calls me. So if she was calling, it had to be about him. Her voice was soft, too soft, "Domonique, your Dad is really sick. The doctors told me to call you they don't think he's going to make it through the night." Silence. Complete silence. In my head, no, no. I'm not ready for this and she gave me the hospital name. I was in the middle of picking up my kids. But really, I was trying to avoid what I thought was coming. I asked, "Do you think he'll make it till morning? I can come first thing?" The old me, she would've dropped everything, found someone to get the kids and rushed to the hospital. But that girl, she had died and I needed a moment to breathe, to wrap my mind around this. I prayed, "God help me forgive him. Please give me another chance." Because even after everything, even after the silence, the pain, the public apology, the doubt— I was still his daughter. Still that little girl who just wanted her daddy.

I walked into the hospital room unannounced, unexpected and the look on his face said it all. He was shock, like he'd seen a ghost or maybe a prayer answered. I hadn't seen my daddy in what felt like two years. But in that moment, time folded in on itself. "**Hey, Daddy**." Just hearing that word, *"Daddy."* It was like it breathed a little more life into him. His eyes lit up. His body weak just moments before, seemed to sit up straighter. I started talking to him like nothing had changed. Like we hadn't lost time. Like we hadn't lost *us* and just like always…he started laughing at my jokes. That laugh I knew so well. That laugh that used to make me feel like the most special girl in the world. His energy shifted. He looked alive, not like the man the doctors said wouldn't make it through the night. That's when I realized, it wasn't the disease that was killing my daddy. It was the heartbreak, it was the weight of our broken relationship. We spent hours together in that room, no cameras and no audience. It was just me and him. He began to apologize, over and over. Not for show, but from his soul and for the first time I began to really forgive him. Not because he earned it, but because I needed it that little girl in me still believed in her daddy and that woman in me was ready to heal.

I kissed my daddy goodbye, softly and gently. **"I'll call later to check on you."** I'm no doctor, but I had faith. Faith that he was going to be okay; because for the first time in a long time, we were okay. As I stepped out of the room, his wife followed behind me. We stood just outside the hospital doors. That's when she told me everything. Her voice was low, careful like she was trying not to break me. She said, **"Your Dad had an STD,** curable; but it went untreated for what the doctors believe was over 20 years." It had reached his brain and he has been having mini strokes. The part of the brain that gives you a conscience, it was gone. Suddenly, so much made sense, the outbursts and the extremes. The way he pushed boundaries as the "most controversial man" in entertainment for over 50 years. He didn't even realize he was taking it too far. Then she said the words that hit the hardest, **"He has stage 4 heart failure."** Just like that, my own heart cracked. Not just because of the diagnosis, but because I realized it wasn't just his body that was failing. It was everything that had gone untreated. The pain, the silence, the pride, and the years, and yet, I had just seen him laugh. I had just seen him *live* even if just for a moment. Sometimes, love is the medicine and forgiveness is the cure, we never knew we needed. I started checking in regularly. Calling to make sure he took his meds and asking if he ate. Little by little, he started sounding like *himself* again. That day at the hospital, talking with his wife opened my eyes. She had a lot on her plate. More than I ever realized. It wasn't fair for her to carry that weight alone. Because behind the

114

voice of *The Cussing Pastor* was a man who had become hard to live with; a man who took advantage of kindness. A man who could be verbally abusive, stubborn, and selfish. She was dealing with all of it, quietly. Then there were the other women. The ones who disrespected their marriage in every way, my daddy allowed. She stayed, and she endured. Now with heart failure slowing him down, he wasn't the same man who once lit up stages and stirred controversy. He moved slower, became tired quicker. His shows were now done from home. Even walking up the stairs took too much out of him. Hospital visits became more frequent. I made it my business to be there. No matter what had happened before, no matter how broken we had been, I was still his daughter. Still that "Daddy's girl." This time, I wasn't going to miss the moments that mattered. We celebrated daddy's birthday in true *Thaddeus Matthews* fashion. Big, bold and blue. He threw himself a show. Not just any show, a **big blue show**, full of lights, laughter, and legacy. Like always, he rolled out the red carpet for his baby girl. I walked in like I owned the room, **bad to the gods,** because I knew all eyes would be on *his daughter*. Just like my daddy, I loved to dress, to make a statement. To walk in a room and leave it talking, my sister was there, too. Both of us his girls were laughing, dancing, and soaking up every second with our father. We didn't know, we couldn't have known that, it would be the last birthday we'd ever celebrate with him. But that night was magical, it was joy. It was *him* and for a moment, we weren't thinking about hospitals or heart failure. We were just daughters, celebrating the man who gave us his name, his fire, and his unforgettable presence. God had started doing His *thang* with me and baby, it was showing. I was finally at a job that matched my standards **my field, my pay, and my pace.** A big, beautiful office with my name on the door and my own parking spot out front. I quit **two jobs** in one day, I walked away with my head high. I could feel God's presence all around me, whispering, **"I told you I got you."** That entrepreneur girl in me, the one who used to dream big, she had dimmed under the weight of all the hurt with my father, but I never let go of my tax business. That business carried me through more than just bills, it carried my *faith.* One of the jobs I left, they had fired me once before, but when they found out who my father was, they got scared. Scared of retaliation, because the death threats were loud. Daddy had started solving a murder case, a famous rapper in South Memphis. When daddy stirred the pot, the whole city felt it. Meanwhile, I was adjusting to my oldest being away at college. Proud, but missing him like crazy and then a blow-up with my youngest son's father. It was so big, until the police were called. All because I put him on child support and I found out he had been using my son's tablet to GPS track us. Without my knowledge, that was his punishment to me leaving me to raise our son alone. But I said, "Hey, I raised one. I can do it again." I was back in therapy, back to choosing *me.* Sleeping peacefully at night, not worried about being cheated on, lied to, or manipulated. This time I wasn't just surviving, I was healing, I was thriving. I was finally walking in the purpose God had for me all along. For the first time in my life, I was watching my **mother** be loved *correctly.*

Not just as a woman, but as a girl soft, protected, and adored. She started opening up to me, telling me stories about her and my father, and the pain she carried from her own father. I realized, I didn't just mirror her in looks. **I was her** and for the first time, I could appreciate that. More importantly, I could *understand* her while she was living in bliss, my father's world was slowly crumbling. His wife had reached her limit, tired of being his caregiver, his emotional punching bag, and his lifeline. She had saved him from strokes, from heart attacks, and from himself. The man she was saving had become hard to love. That *Cussing Pastor* persona had taken over the real Thaddeus Matthews. He was stubborn, selfish, verbally abusive and still entertaining other women who disrespected their marriage in every way he allowed. Then came the family meeting. Daddy called me and my sister over, for once, he wasn't performing. He was facing reality. His heart failure had reached its final stage. Now labeled **chronic**. His heart was only working at **20%**. He was losing his hearing. His body was filling with fluid and the pain was daily. Years of ignoring doctors, skipping meds, never taking time off from the show, it had all caught up. He knew his time here was becoming limited. So I asked the question he kept dancing around, "So if something does happen, how do you want your funeral?" **"What the hell, Domonique! I'm not dead yet!"** We all laughed. I cracked a smile. "Daddy, we gotta be real. That's why we're here, right? I mean, I don't even know what pastor to call. You might need to record your own eulogy and do it yourself," more laughter. Then, his voice turned serious. **"Pastor Floyd is to do my eulogy** and E.H. Ford is the only one to get my body." Just like that, we were really doing it. Planning his funeral while he was still here. It was surreal, but it was necessary. Because even in the hardest moments, we were still his daughters and he was still our daddy. My daddy's wife had finally reached her breaking point. You could feel it in the air, **divorce** was circling like a storm cloud. Through it all, our relationship was getting closer and I truly respected her, because to love a man like my daddy, you had to be built different. You had to love past ego, past pride, and past pain. Me and my sister used to joke and call her **Jesus Jr.**, because *we couldn't have done it.* Not with the way he talked, the way he moved, and the way he *was*. Then the fights started spilling out **right there on social media.** What my daddy once did to me, he was now doing to her. I remember their wedding. I remember looking at her and wondering, *"Does she really know what she's getting herself into?"* To me, she didn't look happy, but she did loved him. I'll never forget the reception his ex-girlfriends and side women sitting in the crowd bold as ever. I asked one of them, **"What are y'all doing here?"** She smiled and said, **"Your daddy will always be my friend."** Whew! Now years later, his wife had decided to move out. Daddy, ran to Facebook every chance he got. **Lord, the embarrassment.** He'd go live. Then she'd go live. He'd go live again and she'd follow right behind. I finally texted them both, "Can this family act normal for once? Why does all our business have to be public?" The fans were eating it up, every post, every video, and every messy moment. Daddy had turned his

118

wife into a version of *himself;* except instead of exposing others, **she was exposing him.** I just sat there, watching the man I loved and the woman who tried to love him tear each other apart in front of the world. All I could do was shake my head and pray we would find peace before the story ended.

With all the drama swirling through the city, for once, **nobody had dragged me into it** and I appreciated that. Father's Day came around, and in the past, I spent every single one with my daddy except for that year and a half we weren't speaking. This year with all the noise on social media between him and his wife, I honestly didn't care to do it. After church with my mom, she looked at me and asked, "You talked to your daddy? Are you taking him out today?" I shrugged, "I put up a post. I don't know about going out." She gave me that *look,* that *mama look,* and said, "Girl, call your Daddy. He's sick. You don't want to regret it," and she was right. Daddy was living alone now. His wife who once waited on him hand and foot was gone and I knew he was over there struggling. Still, I called regularly, I made sure he took his meds. I made sure he ate and more times than I liked, I was DoorDashing food to the house. On the drive home, I called, "Happy Father's Day, Daddy. What you up to?" His voice sounded tired, low, and worn, "Thank you baby, just leaving church?" "Of course," I asked, "You hungry? Want me to send you something?" He sighed, "Nah you can just cash app me. I'll stop and grab something." I made more small talk, and said okay. I will send it now. I felt I could hear the sadness in his voice, and this wasn't our usual type of Father's Day. As I kept

119

driving, I believe God spoke to me and I immediately called him back. "Daddy what part of town are you on? Do you wanna meet me at Red Pier?" You could hear the excitement in his voice, as we both shared the love for seafood.

Back in the days, this club named "Blu" used to have all you can eat crab legs on Friday's and every Friday night until they close, that was our thing to do together. He was my drink buddy, I would cock block the women from him, and he would cock block the men from me. I got to the restaurant first, because I was close to the area. The host picked a table in the middle of the floor, which was no problem for me. Daddy liked to be seen and it was where he could see everything and everyone. I sat there, smoothing my dress, checking my phone, ten minutes passed, then I saw him. At first, I didn't recognize him. My heart skipped, as he walked slowly, leaning heavy on a cane. The man who used to stride into rooms like he owned the air now moved like every step cost him something. He wore a tan suit one that didn't fit, not like the tailored ones he used to wear with pride. No "Cussing Pastor" embroidery on the pocket, just plain fabric hanging off a frame that had lost too much weight. His blue shirt was open at the collar, no tie, no undershirt just skin and bones and a man who couldn't find the strength to care. His shoes were not the polished, his Stacy Adams he used to shine every Sunday morning. These were old, stretched-out, no-name shoes. The kind you wear when your feet are too swollen for anything else. He groaned as he sat down, loud and aching. I rushed to help him, my hands under his arm like I was

120

the parent now. When I sat back down and looked at him, really looked and I had to swallow hard. This was the first time I saw my daddy and knew he wasn't just sick. He was slipping. I remembered a time not long ago, when the doctor wanted to admit him. He fought it, scared like a child. He cried, not from pain, but from fear. I held his hand and whispered our little joke, "Daddy, you gotta stay. So you don't make me an orphan child." He laughed through the tears, and he stayed. But now, sitting across from him, I saw the sickness. The depression, the sadness in his eyes that used to sparkle with mischief, and I knew. I knew that soon, I wouldn't be joking about being an orphan child. I would be one. We talk about his separation, his mental state, and more importantly his health. I was used to people staring at us when we were out to eat, I mean he was Thaddeus Matthews! This time the stare's felt more of horry. After leaving, I call my sister and said sadly, " I think I just had my last Father's Day with Dad." I knew I had to step up. Daddy couldn't take care of himself anymore, and there was no one else. It wasn't even a question, it was just what had to be done. That's what you do when you're a Daddy's Girl. You show up. But Lord, I was already stretched thin. I was the go-to person at work, 120 people depending on me to have the answers, to fix the fires, to keep the ship sailing. Then I'd come home, kick off my heels, and jump straight into toddler time, sticky fingers, bedtime stories, and endless energy. Let's not forget my college baby, out there chasing his football dreams. I was still his anchor, even from miles away. Now, I was adding daddy to the mix. Doctor's appointments, medications, making sure he ate, making sure he felt seen. It was a lot. Some days I felt like I was holding up the whole world with one hand and trying to catch my breath with the other. I didn't complain, I couldn't, because love doesn't always come with convenience. It comes with commitment. Finding time for me? That felt like a luxury I couldn't afford, but I reminded myself, this season won't last forever. Even in the chaos, I'm still standing, still showing up, and still loving hard. Hey… I'm a big girl. The first time I came to clean daddy's house after she left that was the heartbreak I didn't see coming. Not because she was gone, I had made peace with that, but because of what I walked into. Daddy lived in a beautiful four-bedroom house. From the outside you'd never know, but when I opened that door, I was hit with a wave of heat, the sharp sting of urine, and the heavy scent of old age and neglect. My heart dropped. To the right, the dining room had become his studio his little world where he did his show. The table was a mess of microphones, pill bottles, half-eaten plates of food swarming with gnats, and open urine containers like the ones they give hospital patients who can't make it to the bathroom. I stood there frozen. The kitchen was worse, flies every-where, and dishes stacked high in the sink. Counters littered with more food, and more mess. I grabbed the fly swatter, thinking I could handle it. But behind those blinds, it was a war zone. I had to bring out the bug spray and fight like my life depended on it. There were too many, too fast, and too real!

I didn't want to touch anything. I didn't want to believe this was how my Daddy had been living. I was in

122

shock, in pain and in sadness so deep it sat in my chest like a stone. So I did the only thing I could do I turned on my gospel music. Let the voices of praise drown out the ache in my heart. I put on my rubber gloves, wiped my tears, and got to work. Because I'm his daughter, his baby girl and even when it's hard, even when it breaks me, I show up. Now, I was at daddy's beck and call and let me tell you, my daddy didn't play. Every hour on the hour, he was calling, "Take this, take that," but it wasn't like before. Fluid was building up in his body so fast, it was like it was trying to escape any way it could, and I couldn't keep up. I was at work during the day, juggling everything and everyone, and I had no way of knowing if he was actually taking his meds. I'd ask, he'd say yes, but I knew better. The fluid kept building, and so did the bills. He was months behind on rent. The stress of it all was wearing him down, and it was wearing me down, too. Then I saw it, that leg, it was swollen like a water balloon on the side, something I had never seen in my life. I rushed him to the doctor, and of course, he knew what was coming, admission again. I still kept in touch with his wife. I knew she cared, even if they were too angry to speak. When he got admitted, it was like they were treating him like a celebrity trying to hide him from the press, false name and full security. No one could find him unless he wanted them to and then he started letting fans visit. Strangers, people from his show, and from the internet. Every day I'd scroll my timeline during my break at work, and there he was my daddy, in his most vulnerable state, no teeth and crusty feet. Smiling with strangers like he was at a meet-and-greet. They brought him snacks and drinks. They took pictures like it was a party. As for me, I was at the hospital every day, fussing. Begging the nurses to stop letting people in, but they couldn't. He was giving them the info himself. He was taking pictures of his hospital food like he was on vacation. Posting like he was at a resort and I was losing it. I was trying so hard to protect him to care for him and keep his dignity intact. He was making it so hard and still, I showed up that's what Daddy's Girls do! Even when it's messy. Even when it's maddening. Even when it breaks your heart. Our roles had changed. I was no longer just his daughter, I was his protector. The same way I protect my boys and if there's one thing you don't do with me, is mess with my kids.

I was scrolling down my timeline, trying to catch a breath between work and worry, and there it was another post. This time, a video, a dark skin, butch looking woman with thin locs, feeding my Daddy grapes like they were filming a scene out of some low-budget romance flick. I was stunned. Embarrassed. Furious. He was doing the most trying to piss off his wife like some high school boy acting out for attention. The world, they were eating it up, laughing, sharing, and commenting. What was pure entertainment for social media was killing me inside. I knew my daddy was slipping. Losing his grip; but he was too smart to let anyone else see it. He had the doctors and nurses fooled, too. I kept asking for a head scan, but they kept brushing it off. "No need," they said. But I knew better, this wasn't him. After a long day at work, I walked into his hospital room, exhausted and there she was the grape butch lady. Dressed like a man in scrubs like she belonged there. I half-spoke, barely acknowledged her, and made small talk with daddy like she didn't exist. I was annoyed! No, **I was done**. I had already posted from his page, begging fans to stop coming up there and here she was anyways. I sat in the chair, quiet, just listening and then I heard it! She was feeding him gossip about that activist guy who lied on me in that live video, trying to stir the pot. My daddy said, "Yeah, this the first time I've seen you in person." Confirming that he didn't know this girl, I pretended to scroll through my phone, but I was boiling. Another stranger, another boundary crossed, another moment where I had to swallow my pride and hold my tongue for him. Even when he's making it hard, even when he's pushing every button I've got, I'm still his daughter. I was at my wit's end with daddy and his hospital shenanigans. Every day it was something new and then *there she was*. Scrolling my timeline like usual, and boom—**her**. The same chick who had the nerve to comment on my page during that fallout with Daddy, trying to be funny, *"Do you need to borrow $100 until you get paid?"* I never forgot that. Over time, I saw her going back and forth with him on his page, and he even blocked her at one point. But now, she was smiling over my daddy like they were best friends and there he was again, no teeth, feet, legs looking a mess, and she's grinning like she won a prize. That was it, I called his wife. I needed to vent and for the first time, I really understood her. I said, *"I need you to come up here and shut this down."*

I made it to the hospital before she did, so daddy wouldn't suspect a thing. I had no fight left in me. I was tired. Tired of protecting him from himself. Tired of strangers turning his pain into a circus. Then she walked in, six-inch heels, makeup flawless, and her hair wrapped in a bun like a crown. She didn't say much, and she didn't have to, because her presence alone was a statement. Let's just say… after that, nobody else came up to that hospital.

Dear Me,

I see you. I see the tired eyes behind the brave face. The way you carried the weight of the world on your shoulders, juggling work, motherhood, and the chaos of caregiving. I see the way you showed up for Daddy— every single time—even when he made it hard, even when he didn't see how much it was costing you. You did everything you could to protect him. From the world, from strangers, and from himself. You fought battles no one saw, cried tears no one heard, and still managed to smile when he needed you to. You were fierce. You were loyal. You were love in its purest form. I know you questioned yourself. Wondered if you were doing enough? If you were strong enough? If you were seen? Let me tell you now—you were more than enough. You were a warrior in rubber gloves, a guardian in gospel, a daughter who never gave up. You didn't fail him. You honored him. You stood in the gap when no one else could and even when your heart was breaking, you kept showing up. I'm proud of you. I love you.And I want you to rest now. To breathe. To know that you did your part. That your love was loud, and real, and unforgettable. You were—and always will be—Daddy's Girl.

With all my heart,
Me

Chapter Eleven
WHEN LOVE ISN'T ENOUGH

He was miserable, depressed, and couldn't walk. Alone at night, with nothing but his thoughts and the weight of his choices. Now, everything he was going through every ache, every wound, every lonely hour was the result of decisions he made. The fluid in his body had nowhere else to go, so it burst through his skin. His legs opened wide like water balloons that finally gave out. His longtime doctor sat on the edge of the hospital bed and gave it to him straight: **"You need to go to rehab to get better... or you're going to die."** You'd think that would be enough to wake someone up, but not my daddy. My daddy only cared about one thing, his show. Not his health, not his legs, and not the risk of infection that could take him out if he went home too soon. Just the show. His wife and I were exhausted. We tried everything to reason with him. He was in debt, had taken money from people for ads he couldn't run, because he'd been in the hospital and still, he made excuses. Still, he refused the help. The little girl in me cried out, because no matter how difficult he was, no matter how much he got on my nerves, I still needed my daddy!

The next day, his wife brought in his pastor, his best friend. I'll be honest, I was sick of the "Cussing Pastor." Sick of the shame, the embarrassment, and the chaos. I wanted to disappear, move out of Memphis and start over somewhere no one knew me or him. I was tired of our lives being a reality show for the city to laugh at. Daddy was suicidal. The doctors brought in counselors and social workers. Living alone wasn't safe anymore not physically, and not mentally. He was slipping into something darker. The pastor prayed over him. Daddy cried, he confessed that being the "Cussing Pastor" was his biggest downfall that he was living with the guilt of the hurt he caused so many people. Even after all that, the prayers, the tears, the reasoning, my cries, daddy still chose to go home. That's the part that breaks you. When love, effort, and truth still aren't enough to change someone's mind. I was there, I showed up, and I fought for him, because that's what Daddy's Girls do! Even when it hurts. I knew a storm was coming. I could feel it in my bones. The strongest man I knew, my daddy was becoming weak, not just in body, but in spirit. He was giving up, and I wasn't about to sit around and watch it happen. I was angry and tired. So I told myself, I was going to take a step back. I needed space. I couldn't talk to him for a minute. I was being just as stubborn as he was, but guilt wouldn't let me stay away. Daddy went back home, and like clockwork, five nights a week, he was back on his show. Same mic, same fire, and the same chaos. Then I got a call from an old coworker someone from the job I had grown to love. Apparently, gossip was flying about what Daddy was planning to talk about that night on his show. A sensitive topic, a tragedy. Some of our students had stolen a car, crashed it, and died along with innocent people. It was raw. It was painful and daddy was about to make it worse. He had coworkers of mine commenting on his page, and he was back to being the man he swore he wouldn't be, the "Cussing Pastor." I had finally found a career I valued, finally found coworkers who saw me for me, not just his daughter. Now, he was about to mess it all up again. Then the death threats came and I was included. I called him, trying to reason. Pleading with him not to do the topic. But all day, he was online bashing the students, building hype for the show. What I didn't know was that daddy didn't even have all the facts. He didn't know those students had died too and as I tried to talk him down, tried to protect him from himself, again, he was recording me. I didn't know. I was giving him information he didn't have and he was about to use it, against me. That's the part that broke me, not just the betrayal; but the realization that I couldn't protect him anymore. That my love, my loyalty, my tears, they weren't enough to stop the storm. I was still there, still trying and still showing up. That's what Daddy's Girls do! I had his YouTube show playing on my living room TV just background noise while I moved through the house. I went to the back for something, not thinking much of it. Then... I heard my voice. I froze. I walked back into the living room, confused, curious, and there it was—**our private conversation**, playing loud and clear for the entire city to hear. My voice. My words. My pain on his show. I lost it. I flipped my couch. Started punching the walls, screaming, and crying. *"How could he do this to me again? God, why?"* I had protected him, covered for him, and cried for him. Yet, he turned around and used my trust like it was content. Like I was just another segment on his show. I wasn't just hurt, I was shattered, because this wasn't just betrayal; this was public humiliation again. Why wouldn't he protect me like I did him? In that moment, through the rage and the tears, I took to Facebook just like he would. "I Domonique Matthews, denounce myself as Thaddeus Matthews' daughter, I apologize for all the families he has hurt. That's the curse of being a Daddy's Girl. You love hard. Even when it breaks you. The pot was brewing, baby and not just on the stove, I'm talking about life, drama and chaos. The kind of mess that makes you sit back and say, *"Now who summoned this storm?"*

It all started when I hit "post." Yup, I made my denouncement public on Facebook. I said what I said, and I meant every word. I wasn't about to let folks play in my face like I'm some kind of joke. Momma didn't raise no fool. Whew, *chile*, the way things spiraled! I couldn't have scripted it better if I tried. This girl *you know the one* the one who made that slick comment about the $100? She went to the hospital and saw my dad without permission. She decided to go full WWE on Facebook. I'm talking about 12 hours of dragging. She went live not once, not twice, but THREE times. Brought a whole man into the mix just to talk about *me*. Like, girl, do you need a hobby? A job? A hug? The posts were endless. I had to block seven, yes, SEVEN pages between her and that man. I was out here playing whack-a-troll like it was my full-time job. Why all this unnecessary drama? Why me? But deep down, I could feel it. This wasn't just about Facebook beef. This was the universe shaking things up. My life was spiraling from messy to mayhem, and I knew—*something bigger was coming*. Something major and I had to be ready.

Because when you're a daddy's girl, you don't fold. You fix your crown, block the nonsense, and brace yourself for the next chapter.

Even though Daddy's wife had moved out the house, she was still holding it down when it came to his health. She was the one I checked in with, because for a whole month, I didn't speak to my father, not a word. Just quiet updates through her. Honestly, that silence cut deep.
What hurt even more? Daddy sat there and watched me get dragged on Facebook and watched that girl go live, watched the posts, the comments, the chaos and said *nothing*. Not a word in my defense and because of that, his wife wasn't speaking to him, either. The house was quiet, but not the peaceful kind. The kind that screams. Daddy laid in that bed for a month. No meds. Barely eating. Just fading. His body was filling with fluid like it was trying to drown him from the inside out and to me, that wasn't just neglect. That was a slow goodbye. A silent surrender. A suicide attempt in slow motion. We had no choice. He had to go to the hospital and from there, straight to a nursing home. No arguments. No delays. Just reality hitting like a freight train. Meanwhile, his world was collapsing. His rent was months behind. Lights, on the verge of being cut off. The home we once knew was turning into a shell of what it used to be and as for me, I was watching it all fall apart, piece by piece, powerless to stop it. The chaos was loud. Fast. Crushing. I was just a daughter, Daddy's girl trying to hold on to the man who once held the whole world together for me.
So boom, daddy's wife started leaning on this new woman. We'll just call her *Secret Lady,* brown skin, soft-

spoken, and nurturing. Not flashy, not plain, just there. The kind of woman who blends in until suddenly, she's everywhere. She claimed she'd known my father for over 17 years. She said, she knew *all* his secrets. But me, I had never seen her, never heard her name, not even in passing and that made my skin itch. I didn't know if I could trust her. Daddy's wife, she had dirt on her and she was ready to use her like a pawn in this messy game of survival. See, daddy's wife had been holding it down for *years*. Through the cheating, the mental and verbal abuse. The chaos and now, even though they were beefing on Facebook like two teenagers, she was still the one who saved his life. Still the one making sure he didn't drown in his own silence. I understood her dilemma. I really did, because let's be real, we've *all* played the fool for a man before. But Secret Lady? She was stepping into the spotlight. If you asked me, she was the new First Lady. Daddy had her running around like a personal assistant errands, phone calls, appointments and sometimes he was rude to her, even mean. She stayed because she had love for him, too. Maybe not the same kind, but it was there.

To the outside world, it looked like she was in love with him and daddy's wife, she saw it too. She also knew he couldn't do *nothing* with her in the state he was in. So if Secret Lady wanted to play nurse, she was gonna let her; because that meant she could finally breathe. Finally get a piece of her life back and the wildest part is, The Secret Lady and Daddy's wife started getting close. Real close, by reporting back to each other and tag-teaming his care. I used to joke and call them *sister wives*. Behind the laughs, there was tension, especially when Daddy's wife would get on Facebook and start hinting at this *huge* secret she knew about him. The world was eating it up like Sunday dinner. She had made a name for herself. The woman who wasn't scared of daddy. The one who could curse him out and not flinch. The one who met her match and wasn't backing down.

After daddy was swept away by paramedics that day, the silence he left behind was deafening. Silence has a way of speaking, and daddy left something behind that would shake my soul. I met his wife at the house, we were supposed to clean up, and sort through the pieces of his life. I had questions and baby, she had answers. She looked at me with those eyes that had seen too much and said, "You really want to know?" I nodded, heart pounding. She motioned toward his bedroom. "Go look in the lower dresser. I walked slowly, each step heavier than the last. I opened the drawer. Empty, but not really, because what I found wasn't clothes or papers, it was a truth. A truth so raw it made the air thick. A purple dildo. I stood there just staring at it, tears didn't fall right away. They waited, like they knew this moment needed silence first. That dresser didn't hold things it held his biggest secret, his demons, his naked truth. No words. I walked back into the living room in pure shock, my body moving but my mind frozen. I didn't want to believe it, I couldn't. Daddy's wife, she spoke with a softness that cut deeper than any harsh truth ever could. Then she showed me the videos. One of them made me drop to my knees. The shame that filled my body was unexplainable. Not because of what I saw, but because of how long it had been hidden. How long she had known? How long she had lived with it? *Years?* She nodded, quietly with a kind of strength I didn't understand, yet. For years, people made jokes to upset him. They'd tease, poke, and probe and he'd get angry, *furious*. I thought it was just pride, but it wasn't a joke anymore. It was real and it was *him*.

I left that house feeling like my entire life had been a fraud, angry, and sick. I had to pull over on the side of the road and throw up. The images from those videos, they will never leave me. Not because of what he did, but because of how much he hated himself for it. My father had talked so badly about the LGBTQ community. Loudly, and publicly! Now I know, it was a hatred for himself. A war he never stopped fighting and then it started to make sense. Why he had zero respect for women? Why he was cold? Why he never let anyone get too close? He was given up by his mother. Molested by a woman when he was just a child, that pain never left him, it shaped him. It buried him and now, it's burying me!

Dear Me,

I see you. I see the weight you carried that was never yours to hold. The guilt that wrapped itself around your heart like chains, the silence you kept to protect someone you loved more than words could ever explain. I see the tears you cried in secret, the confusion, the shame, the anger you never felt safe enough to express. You were just trying to love your father. You thought that by carrying his burdens, you were helping him. That if you stayed strong enough, quiet enough, loyal enough, maybe the world wouldn't see the cracks. Maybe he wouldn't fall apart. Maybe you could hold it all together. But sweet girl, that was never your job. You were a daughter. Not a savior. Not a shield. Not a secret keeper. Yet, you showed up. You loved him through the silence. You stood in the fire, even when it burned you. You tried to be everything for everyone—daughter, mother, protector, peacekeeper. Still, you kept going. I want you to know: you did nothing wrong. His choices were never your responsibility. His shame was never yours to carry and the guilt you felt? That was love, twisted by pain. You were never weak for feeling broken. You were human. You were hurting and you deserved to be held, not haunted. I'm proud of you for surviving that season. For not letting it harden your heart. For still loving, still hoping, still showing up for your boys, your mother, and even for him. You are not the mistakes of your father. You are not the silence of your past. You are not the shame that tried to bury you. You are light. You are love. You are healing. You are free now.

With all the grace you never gave yourself,
Me

Chapter Twelve
YOU CAN'T MAKE THIS UP

Daddy had been in the hospital for what felt like forever. At first, things were looking up and he was getting stronger, and the doctors were finally ready to release him. Not back home, back to the nursing home. Only daddy didn't want to go back and the nursing home didn't want him either. Then came the video I still don't know how it got out, but after that, everything changed. His room was given up like he was never coming back. We tried me, his wife, the social workers, even his secret lady friend, we all tried to find him another place. Every time they heard his name, it was the same story, "We're full, we're not equipped, we'll call you back," but no one ever did. It was like no one wanted him. I guess God had other plans. Valentine's Day came, and instead of being discharged, daddy was found barely responsive. That's when everything turned. His blood was infected and sepsis. Just like that, he went from being ready to leave to being rushed to the ICU. It was our worst fear coming true. I can't imagine how lonely he must have felt. To be sick, scared, and feeling like the world had turned its back on you. Then something beautiful happened the secret lady got him talking again. Daddy, my Daddy sent me and my sister each a video. He told us Happy Valentine's Day. He told us he loved us and he said he was sorry! Sorry, he hadn't been a better father.

That video... I'll never forget it. His kidneys were failing. The doctors didn't even know where to start so much was going wrong at once. My sister and I, made it to the hospital and when we got there, daddy asked everyone to leave the room. It was just us. Just "his girls." He had never called us that before. Not once in our lives, but in that moment we were his girls and for the first time, we felt it. Daddy's voice was so weak, and his body once strong and full of life was now just skin and bones. Even in that fragile state, he found the strength to speak from his heart. As he began to talk, I tried so hard not to look directly at him. I didn't want him to see the tears that were already falling, no matter how hard I tried to hold them back. He looked at my sister and told her something that shattered me, "You're going to have to be there for her, as if he knew I wasn't going to handle losing him." He was talking about me and he was right. I wasn't ready and I'm still not. Then he turned to my sister and gave her the apology she had deserved for so long. A sincere, heartfelt apology and something strange happened inside me, I felt a weight lift. Maybe because I had carried the guilt of being the "favorite child" for years. Not because I wanted to be, but because that's how it always seemed to others. He made it that way. I used to feel my siblings' pain, even though they didn't really express it, when people acted like I was the only one who mattered to him. Like I was the only one, he saw and even though I cherished our bond, I hated that it made them feel less than being his children. In that moment, watching him give my sister the love and recognition she had longed for, I felt peace. Because for once, it wasn't just about me it was about *us*—his girls.

Even though I was losing him, I was gaining something too, the truth, the healing, and the love that had always been there, even if it hadn't always been spoken. I spent every moment I could at the hospital, sitting by daddy's side, showing him the hundreds of photos we had taken over the years. We always loved a good photo every time we were together, we made sure to capture the moment, smiles, silly faces, and hugs. Those pictures became my lifeline. Then one day, he winced a sharp pain in his stomach. I didn't think much of it at the time just another discomfort in a long list of them. The next day, everything changed. When I came back, the doctors told me daddy was bleeding internally. His heart was barely working maybe 15% at best. His blood was septic. His kidneys were failing and now his stomach was bleeding, too. It felt like his body was shutting down piece by piece. The doctors decided to try dialysis, but not the usual kind his heart was too weak for that. They put him on the slowest dialysis possible, stretching it out over 72 hours. I sat there, watching the machines hum and beep, praying they were buying us more time. Daddy stopped eating. He barely spoke. The sparkle in his eyes was fading. Time wasn't on our side and even though everything pointed to the end, I was still in denial. I kept thinking, *"He's strong. He's come back before. He'll come back again."* Deep down, I knew I was watching my hero fade and yet, I stayed. I held his hand. I showed him more photos. I whispered stories, because even if time was running out, I wanted him to feel loved every second he had left.

I was at home, trying to distract myself doing anything to keep my mind from drifting back to daddy. Then my phone rang, it was him. "Baby, I wanna go live." I looked at the phone confused, *"Why you wanna go live, daddy?"* "I gotta tell everybody how good God has been to me."
I tried to stall him. "Daddy, I don't know if that's a good idea, but I'll be up there soon." When I finally made it to the hospital, I was surprised to see him out of bed, sitting up in a recliner. The shock hit me like a punch to the chest his body looked like a skeleton. So frail, so thin, my heart dropped; but I smiled and I faked it the best I could. He was waiting for me, ready to go live. Still holding on to his faith, his voice, his purpose. I couldn't let him. I gently told him no, trying to keep my voice calm, and steady. "Let's take a picture instead," I said. He agreed. I didn't know then that it would be our last picture together. The last time I'd see that spark in his eyes, even if dimmed by pain. The last time I'd feel his warmth beside me. The last time I'd hear him call me "Baby." Now, that photo means everything. After taking the picture, I did what I always did I tried to make sure daddy looked his best. I found the right angle, softened the lighting, and even checked with his wife before posting it. I wanted to honor him, not embarrass him. "Daddy, what do you want me to say with the picture?" He smirked, weak but still full of that fire, and me as his fiery daughter, "What do you want me to tell 'em you said?" "To everyone who's praying for me, thank you and to everyone who's not, they can kiss my ass." We both laughed. "Yep, say it just like that," he said. So I did.

I posted it not thinking much of it. Just a daughter sharing a moment with her father. I told him I was heading out for the weekend with some friends, just to clear my head. I made him promise to still be here when I got back. I really believed he would be. I thought I had more time. I was still in denial. He had pulled through before, why not again? On the drive home, my phone wouldn't stop ringing. "Are you okay?" "Have you seen Facebook?" The picture had gone viral. Over 500 shares already. I couldn't see the shared comments, so I didn't think much of it. My friends and family were seeing everything and it was bad. People were making jokes, cruel ones. Some even wished death on him. On my daddy, a man who was fighting for his life. Daddy had become the most hated and yet, the most watched man in the city. I understood why. He had hurt a lot of people, including me. The pain he caused wasn't just public, it was personal and while I tried to make sense of everyone's opinions, I couldn't ignore my own heartbreak. There were nights I sat alone, drowning in the waves of shame and confusion. I'd ask myself, *"Would the noise stop when he was gone? Would the attacks finally quiet down?"* Just thinking that brought tears to my eyes. The guilt of wishing for peace through his absence was unbearable. When that picture went viral, I felt exposed. I was glad to be leaving town, heading somewhere no one would recognize me. Somewhere I could breathe without the weight of his name pressing down on my chest. Before I left, daddy's wife told me something that made my stomach turn. People had been scheming on him through his Cash App and he had no clue. It wasn't unusual for his followers to send donations. Daddy had always had a way of drawing people in, even when he was at his worst, but this was different. Someone had been sending him requests for money, writing in the description as if they were *giving* him money and because daddy wasn't in his right mind, barely holding on he was sending it. Almost $800 gone. Just like that! That's when she started digging deeper into his Cash App history. Daddy had been sending money to people just to bring him lunch. A few dollars here, a few dollars there. Then there was a woman the one he tried to play against me on Facebook, calling her his "play daughter." She took an off guard picture of her, telling everyone how she always came to see him to have lunch. He sent her money too. I felt piss off, layered on top of confusion. I didn't know whether to be angry or just sad. Daddy was slipping, and people were taking advantage of him and I was watching it all happen from the sidelines, helpless. I was losing my daddy not just to sickness or shame, but to the world that once cheered for him and now picked him apart. I was losing my mind at the same time. Losing my daddy was like losing the sun in my sky. He was my protector, my guide, and my constant. So when he fell ill, everything in me shifted. I was hurting, confused, and trying to hold it together while the world around me was falling apart. Through his wife, I learned that this play daughter's mother had a long-standing beef with daddy's wife. That caught me off guard. I didn't even realize who her mother was at first. Turns out, she had been following me on Facebook for years commenting on my posts, sliding into my inbox, even calling me once about buying life insurance. She was friendly, familiar. Surprisingly, what I didn't know was that she had been my father's mistress for over 30 years. Through nine marriages, I felt like I was unraveling. I was stunned, hurt, angry, and confused. How could someone who had been so close to me, even in small ways, be tied to such a deep betrayal? Still, I reached out to her. No attitude, no drama. She was kind, even asked if she could visit daddy in the hospital. I told her that wasn't my call, it was up to his wife. Because if I were the wife, and my husband was dying, a side chick showing up would be a hard "No." Eventually, the truth about the Cash App came out. The play daughter explained that when daddy wanted food, she didn't have the money or gas to bring it. So he'd send her money just enough to help and honestly, I believe she cared for him. Maybe not in the way I did, but in her own way and that softened something in me. I'm glad I didn't jump to conclusions. I'm glad I asked questions, because grief is messy, and love especially daddy's kind of love was complicated. Through it all, I'm still his daughter. Still the girl who loved him fiercely and even in the storm of secrets, I choose grace. For him and for me.

I had just come back from a short trip with my girls, Saturday and Sunday. I told myself I needed it. A breather, a break from the noise in my head that never seemed to quiet down. Even in the laughter, the drinks, the music, I couldn't escape. I was there, but not really. I found myself drifting off, staring into nothing, and drinking more than I ever had. Not to celebrate, but to numb to silence the ache in my chest that felt like heartbreak layered on heartbreak. I was trying to escape a reality I couldn't bear to face: life without my father.

Monday came, February 24, 2025, woke up that morning like any other, ready for work, in good spirits, still clinging to hope. I prayed no one would bring up that viral photo of my father, looking so fragile, so unlike the man I knew. But for the first time, my boss usually all business asked me, "How's your father doing?" It caught me off guard. I was grateful he asked, but I gave my usual answer, "We're taking it one day at a time." I was still trying to convince myself he'd pull through. Daddy had taken a turn for the worse. My sister, his wife, secret lady, and I had created a group text to stay connected, to share updates, to hold each other up. My sister and I both had demanding jobs, so the thread was our lifeline. But that morning, something felt off. Noon was approaching, and no one had said a word that silence screamed at me.
I sent a message, "Hey y'all, y'all been quiet today. How my daddy doing?" Not long after, his wife called. I remember picking up the phone, but the details of the call blur. I was walking to my boss's office to get papers signed when I heard the words that froze everything inside me, **"They've put your Daddy on hospice. He's transitioning now. If you want to say goodbye, you need to come."** My brain stopped. My steps slowed. My heart felt like it had left my body. I turned to one of my favorite coworkers and said, almost in disbelief, "My daddy is transitioning." It felt like I was watching myself from outside my body, like a dream I couldn't wake up from. I reached my boss's office. He looked at me and asked, "What is it?" I said, "My daddy is transitioning."

I don't remember walking back to my office, but somehow I got there. I stood blank, unable to think. Then three of my favorite coworkers walked in, closed the door, and asked, "What do you need us to do?" I couldn't answer. I was lost. I couldn't cry. I just said, "Put the money up. I gotta go." One of them asked, "Do you need one of us to drive?" Still blank, still trying to pull it together. It was like my outer self was whispering, **"Domonique, you got this."** I grabbed my backpack and keys and walked out the door. In the car, it hit me, I couldn't breathe, I started to hyperventilate. The reality was crashing in, my daddy, my hero, was leaving.

It felt like I was trapped in a movie I couldn't pause, or a nightmare I couldn't wake up from. Everything around me moved, but I was frozen in disbelief. This couldn't be real. On the way to the hospital, I called my older sister, my mom's daughter who quickly reached out to my closest friends. I couldn't cry, I couldn't think. All I knew was, *I have to get there.* When I arrived, the hospital felt different. The hallway to the ICU was long and empty, the floors gleaming under a strange light that made everything feel surreal. I walked slowly, feeling the eyes of strangers on me, but I couldn't look back. I reached the room. Nurses were already watching from the counter. A white curtain covered the doorway, hiding what I wasn't ready to see. I froze. Tears began to fall, uncontrollably. My heart screamed, *"I can't do this. This isn't happening."* His wife called out, "Domonique, why are you just standing there? Come in." I stepped inside, and my eyes went straight to daddy. He was conscious, but struggling, gasping for breath through the oxygen machine. His eyes locked onto mine, and the tears poured harder. He mouthed, *I love you.* My heart shattered. Through the sobs, I whispered, *I love you too.* He never looked away, as if memorizing my face, holding onto me with everything he had left. He kept trying to speak, but all he could say was *I love you.* I held his hand tightly, refusing to let go. My older sister came in and stood behind me. We both reached out, two little girls holding their daddy's hand, needing him more than ever. I held daddy's hand, staring into his eyes, trying to memorize every detail. He mouthed, *"I'm sorry,"* to both me and my sister. That broke me. My sister wrapped her arms around me and whispered to him, *"It's okay to go. I'll take care of her."* A single tear rolled down his cheek.

Trying to be strong, I stepped away so my nephews could have their turn. I went out to FaceTime my oldest son, away at college, giving him the chance to say goodbye. I held the phone to daddy's face, letting them share one last moment. Me and my sister began calling every family member we could, giving them the chance to say their goodbyes, but time wasn't on our side. After the calls, I went right back to daddy. I held his hand, watched him, just trying to be there. Then his wife told the nurse they could bring in the medicine. In my head, the memories flooded in things we hadn't done yet. Daddy would never walk me down the aisle. We used to laugh about it, and I'd tease him that he wouldn't meet the guy until the wedding day so he wouldn't scare him off. I joked that he'd cry through the whole ceremony. Now, he wouldn't get the chance. I was losing my hero, my daddy. Jesus, this hurts. Jesus, so bad. The nurse came in. Daddy wouldn't take his eyes off me. His fragile hand clung to mine and my sister's so tightly. I saw the fear in his eyes. Then they pushed the medicine into his IV, five minutes. He never closed his eyes. He never looked away from me. He held my hand until the very end. Then... he was gone.

At exactly 2:25 p.m., my world shattered. Still holding my hand, his eyes open but fading, I watched my hero, my superman take his final breath. The man who taught me strength, who made me feel safe in every storm was slipping away. I reached for his glasses, the ones he wore every day, and gently laid my head on his chest. The tears came, just like they had so many times before, but this time they carried a weight I couldn't bear. I caressed his arms, memorizing the feel of his skin as it began to turn cold. I wasn't ready. I'll never be ready. I pulled out my phone and played my favorite gospel song, *Brighten Up My Darkest Night*, hoping for one last sacred moment with him. Just me, daddy, and God. But then, *"ding"* a text, "My Condolences." How? How did anyone already know? I looked around the room, confused and angry. One of the nurses must have posted something. I turned to his wife and said, "You have to tell social media now, before they do." Daddy hadn't even been gone ten minutes, and already the noise was starting. The shenanigans. The drama and I knew it was only going to get worse. So I stayed there. My head on his chest, gospel music playing, and crying. My phone lit up with texts, DMs, and calls. I declined them all. I wasn't ready to talk. I wasn't ready to share him with the world, not yet.

The hospital staff was so patient. They gave me what felt like an hour to just sit there, to grieve, to pray, to hold on to the last bit of him I could. I needed God more than ever. Because what was coming next, the funeral, the family, the chaos and I didn't know how I'd survive it. In that moment, I just wanted to be with daddy and I'll carry that moment with me, forever. Everything in me switched into full protection mode. I stood there, silent but fierce, watching the nurse give my daddy his final bath. My eyes didn't leave him. I needed to make sure they handled him with care, with the dignity he deserved. He wasn't just anybody, he was *my* daddy, my protector, and my superman. Then the chaos started. It was breaking news on the local station. My phone was blowing up, texts, calls, and DMs. Daddy had given us clear instructions. We knew what funeral home he wanted, who should handle his body, how he wanted to be honored. We were trying to follow every word, every wish, because that's what love does. The funeral home arrived, and the man said he was trying to beat the news cameras before they caught him rolling daddy out, but just as they were about to zip the body bag, his wife said, "Hold on, one more person wants to say goodbye." I looked at her, irritated. *Who?* Then she came rushing in, the "play daughter," and over my father's lifeless body, she cried out loud, dramatically, **"Daddy! Daddy! I was coming!"** The *audacity*. The *disrespect*. Right in front of his real daughters. I wanted to snatch her bald. I wanted to scream. Instead, I stormed out, pissed off and heartbroken, because I knew now that daddy was gone, so was my shield. The disrespect was going to get louder.

The fake love, the attention-seekers, and the drama. What they didn't know is that the *Matthews* in me had just been activated. Beast mode and they were about to learn real quick, I'm my daddy's child. I carry his fire, his strength, and his legacy and I will protect his name with everything in me.

The circus had already started forming outside the hospital. Cameras, crowds and whispers and we were about to step into my father's spotlight, his final one. The nurse sensing the chaos, walked us through a private corridor to avoid the media and the noise. I moved like a ghost, watching myself from the outside, like I wasn't really there. Everything felt surreal. I just wanted to escape, to breathe, to have a moment that wasn't shared with the world. I drove home to change into something comfortable, hoping to find a sliver of peace. But I was drowning, I wasn't alert. I don't even remember the drive just that somehow, I ended up in my driveway, hands gripping the steering wheel, and screaming. Cursing, and crying, beating the wheel like it owed me answers. "Why didn't you let me take care of you? You were supposed to still be here. How could you just leave me like this?" I felt empty. Heartbroken. Mad. I tried to go inside and change, but the tears wouldn't stop. So I turned to what I knew—Jack. I threw on my Jack Daniel's pullover, grabbed the bottle, and headed to daddy's wife house.
Everyone was there, but I needed *my* people—my sister, my best cousin, and my mother. I needed their strength because mine was slipping. My usual method of pretending to be okay, of showing a brave face, wasn't working. I couldn't even finish a sentence without

breaking down. Then the news cameras arrived. Why? Why now? I didn't want to be seen. I looked a mess. I *felt* a mess. I couldn't speak without sobbing. Here we were another chapter of my life being broadcast, another moment for the world to judge. So I sat there, silent, looking down. Not wanting to be part of it, but staying because my family needed me. Daddy's wife spoke, and I stayed seated, holding back the storm inside me. Because even in grief, even in chaos, I'm still my daddy's girl and I'll carry him with me through every spotlight, every storm, every moment.

I finally made it home that night—drunk, and heartbroken. I stumbled through the door, dropped my keys, and collapsed into the silence. My heart was screaming, but the world was still. I just wanted to wake up from this nightmare, the one where my daddy was gone. I was scared to close my eyes. Every time I did, I saw him alone, in a cold, dark box. My daddy, my protector, my first love. Now, he was somewhere I couldn't reach, couldn't warm, and couldn't comfort. The thought of him being scared broke me in ways I didn't know I could break.

Eventually, exhaustion won. I nodded off, tears still drying on my cheeks. Then a sound, I jump up my heart was racing. I looked around, confused and then I saw it. My DIY accent wall. The one I put up three years ago. The one that had never moved, never peeled, never faltered. It was falling. Piece by piece. Quietly, but deliberately. I stared at it in disbelief. "Daddy?" I whispered. It was like he was there as if he was trying to to tell me something. Like he was reminding me, *"I'm still with you, baby girl."* At 4 a.m., I was on the floor, sobbing, trying to put the wall back together. Not because I cared about the wall, but because it felt like I was trying to hold onto him to keep him close to fix what I couldn't fix. At that moment, I didn't feel alone. I felt him. His presence. His love. His strength. Even in death, my daddy was still holding me up.

I took one day off work, just one, because even in grief, life doesn't pause. But those next few days, I locked myself in my office. I worked. I cried. I worked. I cried. It became a rhythm—one I didn't choose, but one I couldn't escape. Every evening, I drank not to celebrate, not to forget; but to be numb. The protection I always felt for my daddy slowly shifted. It drifted toward his wife. I became fiercely protective of her. She was vulnerable, and the world was loud. Social media was a battlefield. Most people showed love, yes—but some? Some celebrated his death like it was entertainment. Bloggers came for me. Came for her. The noise grew louder and louder. My phone wouldn't stop. DMs, texts and calls. Everyone wanted something. Everyone had something to say and I expressed it all, too much, maybe. But I was dying inside. As a mother, I still had to show face for my boys. I've always been good at pretending to be okay. I know how to wear the mask. My daddy was married nine times, nine. He had a list of side women that could fill a room. They were loud in their grief. Loud in their love. Loud in their disrespect, at least how I saw it. The "play daughter" and her mother, women I had once been cordial with turned cruel. The mother especially, she

claimed her daughter meant more to my daddy than I ever did and that he didn't love me. She claimed that her daughter was better to him than I ever was. It was like being stabbed with words, over and over. When it came time to plan the funeral, I was dead set on keeping it private. I didn't want a spectacle. I didn't want strangers snapping pictures of my daddy's face in a casket and posting it like it was content. I was still trying to protect him, even in death. People didn't get it, they called me a brat, said I was being dramatic; as if I didn't have reasons. As if they knew what it felt like to carry the weight of his legacy, the pain of his mistakes, and the love that never wavered. My worst nightmare was seeing his face on social media, surrounded by hashtags and fake tears. The sex tape, the women, the wild outbursts on live none of that was all he was; but it was all people wanted to remember and I couldn't let that be the final chapter. Even his enemies were in my inbox, apologizing and sending condolences. I wasn't here for it. I didn't respond the way they wanted, so they turned on me and went live. Some posted about me, and tried to make me the villain. I didn't care. I was in **beast mode**. Mad at the world, mad at God, mad at him, and mad that he left me. I lost my biggest headache, my biggest protector, my biggest problem and still, with everything he was mine.
All he left behind were his problems and a bunch of sensitive ass people who wanted to use his name for clout. People who never had to sacrifice their lives for him, like I did.

We met at his wife's house to plan the funeral and there were orders **his orders** about who was to preach his eulogy. I wouldn't have wanted it any other way. His best friend, his pastor. The same man whose daddy's wife would call the hospital to pray for my daddy. The same man who would call me when me and daddy were at war, just to pray for peace. He understood my love for my father. He understood my father's demons, because he had fought the same ones. He gathered me and my older sister and asked, "Is there anything you want me to say in the eulogy?" I didn't hesitate. "I need you to humanize my father," because people forgot. They forgot the good. They forgot the man who loved hard, who gave everything, who was flawed but real. The controversy, the fights, the tape; it had all overshadowed the man I loved so deeply. I needed the world to see him the way I did. Not perfect. But mines. This was my daddy's final show. I was determined it wouldn't be messy not like the chaos people expected. I watched social media like a hawk. People were scared to come. Whispering about drama, predicting fights, assuming the funeral would be as wild as his life. But I wasn't having it. Daddy's wife had an insurance policy through her job, and she paid for everything. I tried to help, however I could whether it was money, support, or just being present. Her nerves were shot, and part of me worried for her. I hadn't seen her truly break down, yet. No tears. No collapse. Just silence and strength and I reminded myself, *don't judge how people grieve.* Even when she went live to vent saying things I didn't agree with, in ways I wouldn't have said, I stayed quiet. I didn't clap back. I didn't correct her, because I was still trying to protect her. Like she was family. Like daddy would've wanted me to, but the noise was loud. The women, the bloggers, the fake love, and the messy posts. I wasn't in the right mindset to see anyone who had ever talked bad about me or my father. Not in person. Not at his funeral. So I made the call. I knew who to call for security and he didn't come alone, he brought an army. He asked me, "You want suits or tactical gear?" I didn't hesitate, "Tactical gear." I wanted the world to know, I wasn't playing with nobody over my father. Not today. Not ever. This wasn't just a funeral. It was a statement. A moment. A final act of love and protection. I was going to make sure my daddy was honored, not exploited, and that his legacy was remembered, not ridiculed; because even in death, I was still his daughter. Still fighting for him. Still loving him. Still protecting him.

That night, after the funeral planning, I was drained. Exhausted in a way I sleep couldn't fix. I pulled into my driveway, and my phone buzzed an alert that my package had been delivered. Of course, not where I asked them to leave it, but I didn't see anything. I had ordered mini teddy bears for everyone to throw into the grave instead of roses, because daddy used to call himself **"Thaddy Bear."** I got pallbearer gloves, matching neckties, and a few special items for my baby boy. It was all part of the tribute. All part of the goodbye. But on my porch—**no box**. I checked the garage—**nothing**. So I pulled up the cameras and there it was; a red car pulled up, reversed to the end of my driveway on the passenger side, a dark-skinned, bald-headed, slim man—looked to be in his 50s, with a gray chin beard walked up to my front door, snatched the package, and ran back to the car. I was **mad**

as hell. No, mad wasn't even the word. I felt **violated**. This wasn't just a box. This was **my Daddy's stuff**. His final tribute. His memory and someone stole it like it was nothing. I broke down right there on my lawn. Kicking, screaming, punching the air, and cursing with every word I knew. I was grieving, and now I was robbed. I took to Facebook and posted the video, **clear as day**. Captioned it: "You want something to go viral? Make this viral. Man steals my father's funeral stuff." I didn't expect what came next.

By the next morning, **Fox 13 News** and **Channel 3** were in my inbox asking for interviews. I kept declining. I told them my family had enough spotlight. One reporter wouldn't take no for an answer, the same one who interviewed daddy's wife right after the breaking news of his death. He got in touch with her, and daddy's wife talked me into it. "You know your daddy would want you to say something." So there I was. Sitting in front of a camera, talking about something I didn't even think was newsworthy. Just pain. Just grief. Just trying to honor my father and the bloggers came for me, again. "For someone who didn't want the spotlight, she sure is all over the news." I was damned if I did, and damned if I didn't. I didn't want fame. I didn't want attention. I just wanted it all to be **over**.

The day of the funeral came, and I woke up at 5 a.m. heart heavy, and mind racing. I was in such a low place, but I had just come from such a high one. I had married my mother, and now I was about to bury my father all in the same month. Both ceremonies wrapped in **purple**, the

155

color of royalty, of power, and of pain. But this was **Daddy's final show**, and anyone who knew him knew he was a dresser, sharp, bold, and loud with style. So as his child, I wasn't going to disappoint. I stepped out in a **full gold sequin dress**, shining like the sun he used to be in my life. A long, natural ponytail flowing down my back, and big shades to cover the storm in my eyes. I was dressed to honor him, to represent him and to remind the world who he was. But I was worried, that **Memphis**, the city daddy loved so much, wouldn't show up. That all the noise, the drama, the gossip would keep people away. It was my first time in a funeral car. First time sitting on the front row and in that car, my nerves were getting the best of me. My chest was tight. I felt like I was about to hyperventilate. I knew people were going to talk. They always did. It's hard living in a world where everything you do is judged. But I needed to take the edge off and my sissy had my back. One shot of tequila and it was time. **Beast mode activated.** Time to represent for Daddy. Time to show up like a Matthews. We don't show weakness. We show strength. We show love. We show up. When we arrived, I looked out the window and my heart swelled. A line of people down the entire block. **Memphis showed up.** They came for him, for the man, for the legend, for the flawed, beautiful, unforgettable soul that was my Daddy! Everyone got out of the car, and I sat there for a moment. Breathing. Praying. Trying to get my mind right to show face, because this wasn't just a funeral. As we got closer to the funeral, the tension started to rise. Daddy's wife and the "secret lady" weren't seeing eye to eye. It was quiet, but it was thick. Daddy's wife felt like she was doing too much for someone who was *just a friend.* Even mentioned renting her own car, because she wasn't sure there'd be room in the family vehicles. I stayed out of it. I had enough on my plate, but I felt the shift. Then came the moment. The one that hits different. The one that makes it real. They asked the family to come forward to **close the casket.** Daddy's wife turned around and there she was, **the secret lady.** She was standing at the front, reaching for the casket. Ready to say goodbye. Daddy's wife was **mad**. You could see it in her face. In her body, in the way she froze for a second; because in her eyes that moment was sacred, reserved and now it felt invaded. But for me, I was just trying to breathe. Trying to hold it together. Trying not to let the drama drown out the grief. Because this was **Daddy's final goodbye** and no matter who was there, who was mad, who felt left out, he was gone. We were all just trying to find a way to let go. I stood there, in my gold dress, shades on, heart shattered. Watching the casket close, watching the chapter end, watching the man who raised me, protected me, drove me crazy, and loved me in his own way be laid to rest. In that moment, I didn't care who was mad. I just wanted my Daddy back. I tried my best to be present at the funeral. I really did. It felt surreal—like I was watching someone else's life unfold. I couldn't believe I was really there, saying goodbye to my Daddy. We had **armed guards** at the door, IDs were checked. We had a list of people who were **uninvited** and they didn't know until they got to the door and were turned away. It was strict, but it had to be. This wasn't just a funeral. It was a **production**, a **protection**, a **statement**. The funeral was streamed live on social media and even in that sacred space, I had to deal with **disrespect** from his women, from the so-called play daughter who acted out at the hospital, from the mother with her cruel words. I was trying to hold it together, trying to be strong for Daddy's wife and my older sister. They even had to turn away **your school board leader** at the door and the **grape lady.** She had the nerve to post her **Cash App**, supposedly to collect money for the funeral. I guess, I don't even know anymore. They stole my packages. I was on the news. The bloggers were dragging me. I felt like I was losing my mind. But through all of that—he had a successful final show. People showed up. The city showed up. The love showed up. Now came the hardest part. **Leaving him.** I got in the family car, headed to the burial. My heart was already heavy, but I was trying to hold it together. I opened Facebook—just to distract myself for a moment, just to breathe and there it was.

The reason I hired security.

The reason we had a secret wake.

The reason his viewing was only one hour.

The reason we roped off the casket.

My father's body in a casket going viral.

I screamed! A deep, guttural scream that came from the pit of my soul. I couldn't believe it. After everything I did to protect him, someone still violated him. Violated *us*. Turned our pain into content. Turned our goodbye into a trending moment.

I felt like the world had snatched the last bit of dignity I was trying to preserve We made it to the graveside.

Daddy was making his presence known, I felt it. The wind was wild, blowing like it had something to say. Like it was him, wrapping around me, whispering, *"I'm here, baby girl."*

After Daddy's best friend, his pastor said the final prayer, it was time to go. I couldn't move. I just sat there, frozen. My body was still, but my soul was screaming. I couldn't leave him out there alone. I know what they say —*to be absent from the body is to be present with the Lord*. But I hadn't gotten there yet. My heart wasn't ready. My mind couldn't accept it to me, Daddy was out there in that ground, alone and scared and I couldn't bear it. My family tried to help me up, tried to guide me to say my final goodbye. My knees buckled, I collapsed. I screamed out: **"I can't leave him by himself!"** I didn't want to let go. I didn't want to walk away. I wanted to soak in my tears, drown in them if I had to, I wanted to stay there until the pain made sense. I had done everything to protect him, to honor him, to fight for him and now I had to leave him? It felt like the final betrayal. Even in that moment, surrounded by wind and grief and the weight of goodbye, I knew Daddy was with me. In the wind, in the tears, and in the scream, he was still holding me.

Domonique,

You've walked through fire and still found a way to shine.

You are the daughter of a high-profile father—flawed, loud, unforgettable. A man who didn't always protect you the way you needed, but who loved you in his own way. A man who was your biggest headache, and still, the love of your life.

*You've carried the weight of his legacy on your back, even while grieving. Even while feeling empty. Even while the world watched, judged, and misunderstood. You didn't fold. You didn't run. You stood tall—in true **Matthews style**.*

You help buried your father with honor, with class, with fire. You fought for his dignity when others tried to tear it down. You protected his memory when the world tried to make a spectacle of your pain. You showed up in gold, in strength, in love. Now, you're learning to live without him. It's not easy. Some days feel impossible. But you're doing it. One breath at a time. One tear at a time. One prayer at a time.

You are not just surviving—you are becoming.

Becoming the woman your father would be proud of.

Becoming the woman your family needs.

Becoming the woman who can carry grief and grace in the same breath.

So when the days feel heavy, remember this:

You are your father's daughter.

You are your mother's strength.

You are your own legacy.

And you are never alone.

With love,
Domonique Matthews

Domonique Matthews, with her father, Thaddeus Matthews in his final days.

www.ingramcontent.com/pod-product-compliance
Lightning Source LLC
Chambersburg PA
CBHW051829040426
42447CB00006B/441